W9-BRD-071

Alan L. Ellis, PhD
Editor

Gay Men at Midlife
Age Before Beauty

Pre-publication
REVIEWS,
COMMENTARIES,
EVALUATIONS . . .

"**E**very gay man—young and old—should read this book. In it, Dr. Ellis has assembled a remarkable collection of life stories that are stunning in the insights they reveal about growing older as a gay man.

These men have done it all: survived AIDS; transcended homophobic religious upbringings; loved and lost intimate partners; abandoned careers for spiritual paths; survived discrimination; and much more. Reading their stories is an enchanting experience that allows the reader to absorb a myriad of life's lessons."

Raymond M. Berger, PhD
Professor of Social Work (ret.),
California State University,
Long Beach

"**T**his is a book for all ages. For the young gay man these fifteen brief and sometimes poignant glimpses into midlife offer hope and anticipation of good things to come. Older gay men who think they have 'been there, done that,' will gain useful—and perhaps surprising—insights into their own condition. Most of all, men now entering or in midlife will find comfort and courage as the various authors articulate their struggle to find their way in a sometimes hostile, but often loving world of colleagues, friends, family, and lovers. From a variety of geographic and religious backgrounds (Cuban, Australian, American Midwest, Mormon, Catholic, Buddhist) readers are sure to find a life they can relate to. In short, there is something here for everyone."

Hubert Kennedy, PhD
Research Associate,
Center for Research and Education
in Sexuality,
San Francisco State University

More pre-publication
REVIEWS, COMMENTARIES, EVALUATIONS . . .

"**M**iddle age offers a time to look back on one's life and connection with others and the world to see what is there for one's future and sense of self. Life stories and reflections from gay men in midlife offer the reader a chance to see how they dealt with their interests and desires while living lives that began at a time when being gay was viewed by the dominant culture as at best a handicap, and at worst a criminal offense against morality. The cultural stereotype, even among gay men themselves, presented a life of slow degradation, potential victimization, ever-dwindling sexual experiences, and disconnection from loved ones and the networks that religion provides, with the prospect of middle age depressing, if it can be attained at all. Contrary to this stereotype, the gay men in this volume depict lives of purpose, connection, spirituality, and honesty with themselves and others.

Some of the men fit stereotypes of gender atypicality, others are remarkably typical. Some discovered gay sexuality when young, others only in middle age. Some found connection and support in a gay community of their own devising, others found it with male heterosexual friends, others in religious community and ritual, and almost all maintained close familial ties amidst negotiation about their identity and its meaning. Cuban, Chinese, Mexican, black, white, Catholic, Mormon—American men of variant types present thoughtful vignettes of their lives for scrutiny."

Robert W. Mitchell, PhD
Associate Professor of Psychology, Eastern Kentucky University

"**G**ay Men at Midlife: Age Before Beauty is a provocative collection of stories of fifteen men, told in their own words, about what it means to be a gay man at midlife. The writers are generally forty to sixty years of age with different ethnic, family, religious, and professional backgrounds. The stories that make up the collection cover a wide range of topics, including searches for intimacy and problems of the heart, coping with failing health and HIV, concerns about social support and familial relationships, and the role of religion and spirituality in the men's lives. Many of the chapters focus on the past and present challenges the writers have faced as they have aged, but more important, also discuss the solutions and resolutions the men have reached to cope with their life dilemmas.

This book will be of broad interest, not limited to gay men at midlife, because so many of the issues the men discuss are universal. The joys and sorrows that they have lived confront all people, regardless of gender, sexual orientation, or sexual identity. Many of the writers describe how their perspective on life has changed, and especially how midlife has brought them to new understandings of themselves, their bodies, their loves, and their families. It is an interesting exercise to have people reflect on what it is that has shaped who they are now, and what emerges is a compelling collection of tales of growth as well as frustration and success.

More pre-publication
REVIEWS, COMMENTARIES, EVALUATIONS . . .

For gay men of all ages, however, the book will be particularly interesting and valuable. By and large, their lives have not fit the cultural script that their families and society suggested for them, and at midlife they find themselves left out of a gay cultural script that stresses youth, beauty, and fast living. Readers are bound to see themselves in the stories of how internalized homophobia led some men to consider suicide, or even to academic and career success; how some handled the delicate task of coming out to parents and friends, and how some have rejected the external measures of success of their youth in favor of internal standards for affirmation and self-esteem. The stories are certainly entertaining, but more than that, they teach and inform. For entertainment, insight, and inspiration, there is little more that one can ask from a collection of stories."

Allen M. Omoto, PhD
Associate Professor,
Psychology,
Claremont Graduate University,
Claremont, CA

HPP

Harrington Park Press®
An Imprint of The Haworth Press, Inc.
New York • London • Oxford

Gay Men at Midlife
Age Before Beauty

HAWORTH Gay & Lesbian Studies
John P. De Cecco, PhD
Editor in Chief

Gay Men at Midlife
Age Before Beauty

Alan L. Ellis, PhD
Editor

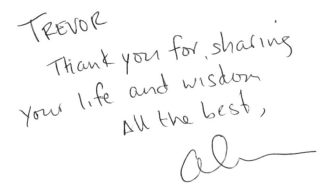

TREVOR
Thank you for sharing your life and wisdom
All the best,
Alan

HPP

Harrington Park Press®
An Imprint of The Haworth Press, Inc.
New York • London • Oxford

Published by

Harrington Park Press®, an imprint of The Haworth Press, Inc., 10 Alice Street, Binghamton, NY 13904-1580.

Cover design by Marylouise E. Doyle.

Library of Congress Cataloging-in-Publication Data

Gay men at midlife : age before beauty / [edited by] Alan L. Ellis.
    p. cm.
    Includes bibliographical references.
    ISBN 1-56023-979-4 (hard : alk. paper) — ISBN 1-56023-980-8 (soft : alk. paper)
    1. Middle aged gay men—Attitudes. 2. Middle aged gay men—Psychology. 3. Middle aged gay men—Mortality. 4. Self-esteem in men. I. Ellis, Alan L.

HQ76.14 .G39 2000
305.244—dc21

00-033535

To the memories of Tom Baranauskas,
Paul Edward Johnson, Arthur Fisher, Dan Mynear,
Steve Gallagher, and the many others who didn't get the chance
to experience life as gay men in their middle years.

CONTENTS

ABOUT THE EDITOR

Alan L. Ellis, PhD, is the author of several books, including *Sexual Identity on the Job: Issues and Services* (Haworth), *A Family and Friend's Guide to Sexual Orientation,* and *A Manager's Guide to Sexual Orientation in the Workplace.* He is also the author of numerous articles and chapters, including the chapter on sexual orientation in the just-released graduate-level textbook *Psychological Perspectives on Human Sexuality.* He is currently co-chair of the Harvey Milk Institute in San Francisco, the largest community-based queer studies program on the planet.

Dr. Ellis is a member of the editorial boards of the *Journal of Homosexuality* and the *Journal of Gay & Lesbian Social Services.* He is Senior Research Associate at the Center for Research and Education in Sexuality (CERES) at San Francisco State University. He received his PhD in psychology from the University of Illinois at Urbana/Champaign.

CONTRIBUTORS

Kevin G. Barnhurst, PhD, teaches media studies at the University of Illinois–Chicago and serves on the National Research Advisory Board for GLAAD.

Christopher K. Bramwell, MA, is based in Washington, DC, and is an evaluation consultant for international clients. He recently completed his graduate degree at Harvard University.

Armand R. Cerbone, PhD, is a psychologist in private practice in Chicago. He is a recipient of the Distinguished Professional Contribution Award of the Society for the Psychological Study of Lesbian, Gay, and Bisexual Issues of the American Psychological Association.

Stephen W. Goodin is a Wide Area Network (WAN) engineer for a Fortune 500 financial services organization in Marin County, California.

Mark M. Harris, PhD, is a psychologist. He is senior staff member at the Counseling Service of the University of Iowa.

Alejandro Medina-Bermúdez, PhD (candidate), teaches philosophy and literature at Syracuse University in Madrid, Spain.

Tom Moon, MFT, is a psychotherapist in private practice in San Francisco. His popular column, "The Examined Life" appears monthly in the San Francisco edition of *Frontiers.*

George Pierson is a television executive. He has worked for ABC, NBC, HBO, and currently leads a creative group for Discovery Communications in Bethesda, Maryland.

Michael Ross, PhD, is Professor of Public Health and Infectious Diseases at the University of Texas (Houston Health Science Center). He is author of nearly 300 publications, including thirteen books, on sexuality, sexually transmitted diseases, and HIV.

Michael Segovia, MA, is a marketing and public relations manager for a publishing firm in Palo Alto, California. He holds a master of arts degree in clinical psychology.

Jeff Siebert, PhD, is a member of the staff and faculty of the Foundation for "A Course in Miracles" in Roscoe, New York. He has been involved in teaching the course for the past five years.

Trevor Southey is originally from Rhodesia (now Zimbabwe) and is an artist living in the Bay Area. His media are varied and his artistic direction is rooted in the Italian Renaissance while exploring his own experience within the framework of his time.

Craig Watters, PhD (candidate), is a doctoral candidate at Syracuse University, New York, in Social Science, Maxwell School of Citizenship and Public Affairs.

Frank Wong, PhD, a first-generation Asian American, lives with his family (one dog and four cats) in the country, two hours from New York City. Born an activist and trained as a social psychologist, Frank does community-based research that serves ex-offenders as well as the immigrant and refugee communities in New York City.

Acknowledgments

This book represents a collective effort. I wish to thank each of the contributors for their willingness and courage to explore and reveal the challenges and joys they face as gay men over the age of forty. I also wish to thank David Attyah, David Brightman, Steve Filandrinos, Jonathan Ford, Randy Huff, Warren Longmire, Tom Metz, Robert Mitchell, John Saccoman, and Geoffery Weiss for their comments on various drafts of portions of the book. I especially wish to thank John De Cecco for his ongoing support of this and other similar works.

Chapter 1

Introduction: The Beauty of Men

Alan L. Ellis

Everyone was a God, and no one grew old in a single night. No, it took years for that to happen . . .

Andrew Holleran, *Dancer from the Dance*

Dancer from the Dance[1] was published in 1978, and while those of us now in our forties and fifties didn't grow old in a single night, two decades passed, and we did grow older. In those twenty-some-odd years, the gay community matured as well. Considerable progress has been made toward altering many of the negative stereotypes about gay men and other members of the queer community. However, we still live in a homophobic and heterosexist society. When we combine negative biases about homosexuality with similarly nega- tive biases about aging, we are left to confront a societal script for aging gay men that tends to propagate a stereotype of isolated and alienated individuals. It is a script in which isolation, bitterness, and regret multiply with age. One of the choices many of us as gay men face is whether to live out a script that society wishes to impose on us or to empower ourselves to write our own.

Clearly, it's not an easy task. Both straight and gay writers have reinforced the concept of the lonely and bitter aging gay male through- out our lifetimes. Andrew Holleran's recent book *The Beauty of Men*[2] presents a devastating portrait of a fifty-year-old gay male who embodies most, if not all, of the negative characteristics of the stereo- type. Reviews of the book describe the male protagonist as "riddled

1

not only with the guilt of a survivor whose friends have succumbed to AIDS but with a deeper sense of despair at his own homosexuality,"[3] and as a man "who pines for lost youth and to meet again a younger man he had sex with a year ago . . . he thinks intelligently if egocentrically about his life and his plight. He is pathetic."[4]

Not surprisingly, everyone I know who read the book found it depressing. Whereas Holleran's *Dancer from the Dance* had helped me and others to come to terms with our sexuality and even to come out, reading *The Beauty of Men* led to a growing sense of dread about our future. The book reinforces the belief that aging gay men are isolated, bitter, angry, unhappy, alienated, and lonely. Perhaps we should be grateful to Holleran because *The Beauty of Men* and its depressing depiction of an aging gay man forces us to confront our fears of aging.

Internalizing societal fears and beliefs about aging can keep us from questioning the status quo. Ray Berger, the author of *Gay and Gray*,[5] has noted that negative stereotypes are one of the most damaging weapons that a society can wield against devalued and oppressed groups.[6] Negative stereotypes can lead the oppressed to oppress themselves. Most of us can attest to the pain of growing up in a homophobic and heterosexist culture. The negative stereotypes about what it was to be gay required us as younger men either to continue living in fear or confront our own insecurities about who we were. Most of us have struggled to accept our sexuality, and to move beyond the negative stereotypes and beliefs about what it means to be gay. Now, we find ourselves confronting ageism—an ageism that can be particularly virulent when applied to older gay men. If we're lucky, we have largely won the battle against our internalized homophobia just in time to battle internalized beliefs about aging. Many of us, however, are likely to enter middle age still working to liberate ourselves from the effects of growing up in a homophobic and heterosexist society.

Those of us in our forties and fifties came of age in the 1960s and 1970s—a time when the available commentary on gay life was anything but supportive. Until 1973, homosexuality was a diagnosable mental illness, and even after 1973 writers of articles in the mainstream press still felt free to denigrate us. For example, the following review of Edmund White's *States of Desire* was printed in *The New York Times* in 1980:

> They seem to live in a modern-day inferno, where they despise their own aging flesh, where they inflict ceaseless physical and psychological harm on themselves and one another all in the name of happiness.[7]

Unfortunately, comments such as the above were what many of us as young gay men came across as we contemplated and attempted to understand our attraction to other men. Very little information was available and what was available often reinforced the fears that kept us in hiding. It is not surprising that many of us who grew up reading such statements internalized them. At the time, we might have winced at the suggestion that we lived in a modern-day inferno—and possibly noted somewhere in the back of our minds that we apparently "despise our own aging flesh." The effects of these negative beliefs persist and continue to influence our community. For example, young gay men often refer to a glass-paned bar on Castro Street that caters to older gay men (forty-plus) as the "Glass Coffin."

For those of us who carry the scars and wounds of decades of being exposed to antigay sentiment (as well as the loss and grief of two decades of AIDS) the question is how can we respond now in ways that improve our lives as we grow older? In part, this question requires addressing our role as victims of societal oppression. It is important that we give ourselves permission to acknowledge and process the pain and hurt that we feel as a result of having grown up in a culture that rejected us because of our sexual and affectional desires. However, if we remain focused only on our status as victims, we may be more likely to live out the script that a homophobic society has written for us. By continuing our individual struggles to move through the pain, we are more likely to find the strength and ability to write our own scripts. Developing a new script is not easy, but it does offer us the opportunity to create a future that is based on our own desires and hopes.

One of the primary challenges of aging for gay men is that societal measures of success are typically less relevant to gay lives. Traditionally, society has rewarded those who have children and are in culturally sanctioned relationships. However, recent surveys of the population indicate that approximately one in three adults—regardless of sexual orientation—is single. Currently, the majority of gay men age as singles. Despite these realities, there is an ongoing and persistent cultural belief that being single is somehow representative of failure. While many of us have created effective communities and support networks either as couples or singles, we live in a culture that has few ways of celebrating singles. Part of rewriting the script involves creating ways to honor and celebrate everyone, regardless of relationship status.

Society also rewards those who follow traditional career paths—although even that concept is undergoing significant change. Many of us have chosen to step aside from career paths and mainstream lives in order to explore our sexuality and other aspects of ourselves. As a result, we may find ourselves wondering what forms the foundation of our lives. Although mainstream heterosexuals may face similar challenges in their lives, they also tend to encounter greater support for their choices. Those of us (including queers who are straight) who must find our worth outside mainstream society may find the going tougher, but we may also ultimately be stronger for it because it requires us to confront more directly how we define our being.

Based on the findings of several studies looking at gay men over the age of sixty, it appears that, despite the negative stereotypes, most older gay men adapt as well, if not better, to aging than do straight-identified men.[8] The research suggests that, overall, older gay men adjust better than heterosexual men because older gay men have learned to operate independently of traditional societal structures. That is, older gay men have developed coping skills to deal with societal stigma. Because our society tends to stigmatize the elderly, older gay men may be better prepared to cope with that stigma based on their years of living with the stigma of homosexuality. The positive implication of these findings is that we can collectively challenge and alter the debilitating stereotypes and beliefs about older gay men by living individual lives that neutralize those stereotypes. To do so, we may need to individually confront the negative stereotypes and beliefs as they relate to our lives. This can require integrating those aspects of our selves that we believe are weaknesses and learning to accept about ourselves what others may view negatively. This process is often referred to as "shadow work."

Jungian psychology is known for its attention to "shadow work." Shadows are those aspects of ourselves that we dislike and that we have spent most of our lives attempting to ban from consciousness. Ultimately, they slip into consciousness and require that we confront and accept them. Shadow work typically accompanies middle age and often around age forty most of us begin to confront our shadows. In doing so, the hope is that we develop an increasing sense of worth and peace about ourselves. But "shadow work" is not easy. It can force us into some of the most challenging places we have ever been psychologically. Initially, many of us may work even harder to "distract" ourselves from the dark elements of the psyche. Over time, however, the distractions begin to fail. As gay men, we may be more likely to confront our shadows sooner than heterosexuals because heterosexuals can continue to remain distracted by family, career, and the pursuit of societal approbation—from an early age, we have had to question the value of society's acceptance. As painful as that process has been for many of us, it may ultimately benefit us as we must look elsewhere to establish our inherent worth. We may initially transfer our need for approval to other members of the gay community but are likely to find that, as we age, approval that lies outside ourselves is both transient and ultimately unfulfilling.

Shadow work forces us, then, to confront the difficult questions of our lives—whatever they may be for each individual. A host of promises are associated with acknowledging one's shadows. For example, the author of *The Lazy Man's Guide to Enlightenment* writes "all you need do to get free of pain . . . is to be *willing* to be aware of anything that enters your consciousness."[9] Aging reduces the effectiveness of the defenses and distractions that we use to avoid those things that are uncomfortable. From a spiritual perspective, it may be the universe's way of encouraging us to look at the real meaning of our lives. Regardless, however, of one's perspective, middle age is generally accompanied by an intense focus on determining the meaning of one's life.

In *Letters to a Young Poet*, Rilke wrote: "Live the questions now. Perhaps you will then gradually, without noticing, live along some distant day into the answer."[10] Later in those same letters he wrote

". . . let life happen to you. Believe me: life is right, in any case."[11] The essays in this book are about questions that are being lived and lives that are happening. My hope is that by reading about other men's lives, you will encounter experiences, fears, joys, frustrations, and interpretations that help to illuminate your own life. Undoubtedly, some of the stories will resonate more than others with your life. I have chosen to leave the interpretation of each of the stories up to you, the reader, based on your own life experience. I also hope that in these men's stories you will find experiences that help you further explore the challenges and joys of your own life, and encounter the true "beauty of men," regardless of sexual orientation or age.

NOTES

1. Holleran, A. (1978). *Dancer from the Dance.* New York: Plume.

2. Holleran, A. (1996). *The Beauty of Men.* New York: William Morrow & Co.

3. Hollinghurst, A. (June 30, 1996). So I'm Shallow. *The New York Times Book Review* (p. 7).

4. Olson, R. (June 1, 1996). Review of Andrew Holleran's *The Beauty of Men. Booklist* (p. 1643).

5. Berger, R. M. (1996). *Gay and Gray: The Older Homosexual Man.* Binghamton, NY: Harrington Park Press.

6. Berger, R. M. and Kelly, J. J. (1996). Gay men and lesbians grown older. In R. P. Cabaj and T. S. Stein (Eds.), *Textbook of Homosexuality and Mental Health* (p. 306). Washington DC: American Psychiatric Press, Inc.

7. Cowan, P. (February 3, 1980). The Pursuit of Happiness. *The New York Times Book Review* (p. 13).

8. For a review of this research, see Berger, R. M. and Kelly, J. J. (1996). Gay men and lesbians grown older. In R. P. Cabaj and T. S. Stein (Eds.), *Textbook of Homosexuality and Mental Health* (pp. 306-316). Washington, DC: American Psychiatric Press, Inc.

9. Golas, T. (1972). *The Lazy Man's Guide to Enlightenment* (p. 42). Redway, CA: Seed Center.

10. Rilke, R. M. (1934). *Letters to a Young Poet* (p. 35). New York: W. W. Norton & Company, Inc.

11. Ibid., p. 74.

Chapter 2

A Vipassana Romance

Tom Moon

SAMSARA

From earliest childhood, an almost mystical hunger to be close to other males—physically, emotionally, and spiritually—has dominated my life like a force of nature: ancient, impersonal, and elemental. It speaks through me; it uses me; and someday, it will use me up.

In one of my earliest memories—I couldn't have been older than four—I sit on the landing outside my family's apartment on Capp Street in the Mission District of San Francisco with my friend Davey, who's waiting for his father to come home. The door to the building opens and heavy footsteps are heard below. Then I see Davey's father, Sal, a big, sweaty, unshaven Italian fireman, in red suspenders and a dirty T-shirt, bound up the stairs, pick Davey up, throw him in the air, and give him a bear hug while Davey squeals with delight. I stand watching with intense desire, longing for him to pick me up in the same way. Sal looks down at me, pats me on the head, and says, "How are you today, Tommy?" Then he and Davey walk into their apartment and shut the door. I stand on the silent landing, my eyes fixed on that door.

I also remember Marty—the boy I fell in love with when we were both fifteen years of age. I remember pushing our desks together in English class to share a copy of *Romeo and Juliet* as the class read it aloud together, our heads bent over the book within inches of each other. I could smell him, feel the heat of his body, and I became so dizzy and disoriented that I could barely read when my turn came.

Marty was the star swimmer of the school and I tried out for the swim team just to be close to him. I was a poor swimmer and, not surprisingly, didn't make the team, but I did get to take a shower with Marty. Standing naked next to him as we dried ourselves, and snapping his butt with a towel almost made up for not making the team. On the last day of school, we celebrated by jumping into the swimming pool with our clothes on. I then watched him, still dripping, walk up the trail of a hill and over the crest, knowing that I wouldn't see him again until school started again in the fall. Every couple of days all summer long, I returned to the spot where I had last seen him. I stood there longing for him in a mood of black despair, knowing that he'd never know how I felt about him, much less return my feelings. In September, on the first day of school, I was again standing on that spot when he came back over the trail again.

Not that every love was unrequited. After I came out in my twenties I found my soul mate—six times. I had more boyfriends than I can count, and, to date, I've lived with two lovers. But what makes this longing so uncanny is that nothing ever quite sates it. At fifty-one, it remains as elemental and strong as it was when I was fifteen—a power that has to be respected but can never be completely controlled.

The other side of my sexuality was pure animal desire for the bodies of men. Sometimes this coincided with romantic longing, but usually it was completely independent of it. During the now-mythical 1970s, I used to go to the Howard Street Baths in San Francisco on Tuesday—which was Three-Buck Fuck Night. I'd strip and walk up and down the rows of rooms, looking into open doorways for other naked men lying on their bellies. When they were good-looking and signaled that they wanted me to come in, I'd climb on their backs and wallow in their bodies. I'd fuck half a dozen men before going home, and on weekend nights, the number would be two or three times that. A few months ago—now that those fires have cooled a bit—I got out a calculator and tried to estimate the number of men I'd had sex with in this way over the past thirty years. If I can believe my calculations, the total comes to over 10,000. I'm amazed that I came through this riot of sex without contracting HIV. Virtually everyone I knew during that period of my life is now long dead.

But the real showstopper, and in some ways the climax, of my sexual life was my relationship with Wolf—a man I met and lived with

for about five years during my early forties. In Wolf, romantic longing and physical lust came together for me. Wolf was fourteen years
younger than I, a muscular, handsome ex-Marine, and a sought-after
title holder in the leather community of San Francisco. He was half
Caucasian and half Filipino (although he claimed to be half Native
American). The mix gave his face a beautiful combination of strength
and gentleness that drove me wild.

The night I met him—in a South of Market sex club—I was so
stunned that when I came home, I sat and stared out the window for
hours, unable to move. He came to live with me six weeks later and
stayed just under five years. For a long time, he was absolutely
devoted to me in every way, and I experienced the union of romantic
love and lust that I had longed to feel all my life.

But toward the end of our relationship, he began to feel restless,
and responded to that by becoming increasingly verbally abusive
toward me. In the end he was actually threatening, and I was afraid to
be alone with him. One evening in September 1995, while we were
standing in line for a movie, he walked away from me because he was
angry that I hadn't heard him ask me if I wanted some popcorn. He
never came home again. In the weeks that followed, I discovered that
he had at least two other lovers, and that he had moved in with one of
them—a man he'd always described as his "best friend." As I
emerged from my romantic delusions, I began to realize that virtually
everything he'd ever told me about himself was untrue, and that I'd
been in love with a pathological liar for five years.

I was forty-seven years old.

AWAKENING

The year after Wolf's departure was one of the most difficult in my
life, but I look back on it now as the time when grace appeared in my
life.

About ten days after he left, I went up to Spirit Rock Meditation
Center in Marin County to spend a day learning and practicing
Vipassana meditation, the primary meditation practice that the Buddha taught to his disciples twenty-five centuries ago. I had dabbled in
various forms of yoga and meditation for decades, but I took up this

practice with an urgency, even a desperation, that I'd never felt before.

The pain of loss and betrayal drove me inward, and the interior landscape began to open for me. In my late forties, I finally found myself leaving behind my sexual adolescence. I discovered the secret that there is a great gift to be found in not scratching every itch that presents itself. Most of us, for most of our lives, are more or less held captive by our desires. We unthinkingly live out the cycle of wanting, striving, and getting, and then wanting something new. Naively and forlornly, we believe that our happiness will be found in gratifying our desires. Virtually every human being on the planet is held in the grip of this delusion. What the Buddha's enlightenment revealed to him was that the truth is actually the opposite—the pursuit of gratification not only doesn't lead to happiness, but is in fact the root cause of our suffering. Our craving, our thirst, is inherently painful, and the more we feed it, the more it grows. Every gratified desire leads to more desire—the process is eternal and futile.

The great opportunity that aging presents is the possibility of understanding this truth and getting off the unconscious, mechanical treadmill of desire. When we're young, desire and lust are consuming, and we're too restless and agitated to have much appetite for contemplation. The cooling of youthful passions and the slowing of the body may be a cue from nature to go deeper, to look below the surface of things and to find that which abides with us when all else falls away. It's the cooling that aging brings that also gives us the capacity to be still enough to look within. Traditionally, aging has been seen as the period in our lives when we can develop *wisdom*.

My experience suggests that those who don't begin to look within find the experience of aging as nightmarish—a losing struggle against the long, slow slide of bodily decline. The struggle is especially difficult for modern Americans in a culture that worships all things youthful, and especially challenging for gay men, because the dominant gay culture lives in a dream of perpetual adolescence.

When I took up the daily practice of *Vipassana,* I found my life changing in other ways. I stopped drinking coffee, adopted a healthier diet, and also began a daily practice of Hatha yoga exercises to support my meditation. I discovered the value of extended meditation retreats. Soon most of my vacations were seven- and ten-day retreats in which I meditated from early morning until bedtime. In these retreats, I was able to experience depths of existence that I had never before suspected. I began to experience the kind of mystical experiences that previously I had only read about in books.

At first my sexuality was untouched by all of these changes. After Wolf left, I returned to the way I was accustomed to behaving whenever I was single. I started dating and looking for his replacement, and also had a lot of casual and anonymous sex. Soon, however, my spiritual life began to conflict with my sexual life. In meditation, I noticed that most of my mental agitation originated in my sexual behavior, and that it was far easier for me to devote myself to spiritual practices when I wasn't spending most of my free time going out to chase guys. For the better part of 1998 I was celibate, and I was surprised to discover that I felt happier, more contented, and more alive—without the constant distraction of sex.

LILA

That isn't to say that sexuality completely disappeared from my life, only that not acting on my desires gave me an opportunity to explore them in meditation with greater clarity.

Over the New Year's holiday marking the beginning of 1999, I attended an eight-day meditation at Spirit Rock. On the first night of the retreat, when we all had gathered in the dining hall for dinner, one man caught my attention. I knew nothing about him except that his name was Adam, and that he wore a wedding ring and a stud in his right ear. He was a tall, broad-shouldered athletic man, about thirty-two years old. He was starting to lose his brown hair, and was careless about combing what remained, so it fell in unkempt curls over his head and down his long neck. He had a handsome, clean-shaven face, deep blue eyes, and a broad, generous smile. Throughout the retreat, he wore baggy jeans, flannel shirts, and a green ski cap. He walked with his hands stuffed in his pockets. His walk was more like a glide and there was a kind of "Aw, shucks" boyish masculinity about him that captured me.

For seven days and nights, all one hundred of us were in complete silence. We meditated from 6:15 in the morning until 9:30 at night.

Our schedule was to sit together in the meditation hall for forty-five minutes, go out and do a walking meditation for forty-five minutes, then return to sit again. We repeated the cycle all day and all evening until bedtime.

I had come to the retreat to experience inner peace and calm, but instead found that Adam filled my mind. To support our inward focus, we were encouraged to avoid even making eye contact with one another, and most people walked and ate with their eyes carefully averted. But I couldn't keep my eyes off Adam. I watched him furtively in the dining hall. I watched him as he walked. In the middle of sittings, I would open my eyes and look across the meditation hall at him as he sat cross-legged on his cushion. During the midday meal, I watched him take his plate outside and sit on a rock near a creek and hunch over his plate to eat. After the meal, I watched him stretch out and sleep under the sun. He wore a ski jacket when he slept and kept his arms folded under his chest. It was a cold, frosty winter. An hour or two of fifty-degree weather and sunlight were all we had, and he took full advantage of the opportunity to be outdoors.

I watched him yawn and stretch when we stood up after sittings, and bend over and touch his feet with his hands. I watched him slowly glide over a trail during the walking meditations, his head bowed, deep in inward absorption. I watched him untie the green shoelaces of his big tennis shoes when we came back into the hall. I watched him lower his round butt back onto the cushion, and listened to his deep, sonorous breathing, occasionally heard him clear his throat.

We all had jobs to do during the retreat to help maintain the community, and Adam's job was to wash the dishes after the morning meal. As he rolled up his sleeves, I savored the thick black hair on his muscled forearms and the veins that stood out on his big hands. He put on an apron and tied it behind his back, then plunged into his work.

Adam! Whenever he came into my field of vision, my heart leaped with excitement. I loved him; I longed for him to look at me, to touch me, to enfold me in his arms, to love me in return.

Adam! He was my mantra, the single-pointed focus of my meditation. I told myself not to look at him, to keep my eyes away from him, but it was no use. Whenever I closed my eyes and meditated, there he was in my heart, smiling boyishly, walking, tying his shoes, eating his food on the rock by the creek.

Adam! There was no escape, nothing to distract me. Longing for him filled every cell of my being. I breathed longing. I became an incarnation of longing. Soon the taste of longing in my mouth, the ache of it in my heart, and the tightness of it in my chest were my entire world.

And then it was as if I could see, standing behind him, everyone I had ever longed for in my life. Sal was there and Marty and Wolf and the 10,000. And then I saw the longing at the core of all human beings, and of all life—the futile longing that brings all beings into the suffering of embodied existence. I remember thinking that there is truly no escape from Schopenhauer's ontology of hopelessness. Sweet agony of longing! Cold stab of despair!

Adam! On New Year's Eve, I sat slumped in the hall, in a mood of bleak loneliness. Was the Buddha's promise that there could be a cessation of suffering through these practices just another delusion? How could I ever cease to suffer when the only thing that could end my suffering was the love of a young man on the other side of the hall who didn't know I existed and would never return my affection?

I watched grace unfold in meditation as the true object of my longing gently separated itself from Adam. If I had longed for so many in my life, then it was a delusion to think that each alone was the thing I longed for. No, what I pined for clearly originated inside myself, and was only projected onto these boys, these men.

But what was that?

My mind focused its attention directly on that love, that happiness, that light that I saw shining in Adam's face and Marty's face, and in the faces of all the others. A clear, shining light. There was a shock of recognition. I realized that I was looking into a mirror. The light in my own heart smiled back at me and winked. I laughed at the delicious irony; at the core of this longing was the truth that what I longed for and despaired of ever possessing was, in fact, the one and only thing in this life that I can never lose. And in that light in my own heart, the heart of Adam appeared, and then Marty's heart, and then the hearts of all beings—the one heart that plays at being many hearts, that loses and seeks and finds and loses itself again eternally in the vast play of consciousness, *lila*, that we mistake for a solid world.

My suffering, for that moment, dissolved in a silent song of freedom and joy, and when the New Year arrived, I welcomed it with gratitude.

At the end of the retreat, we ended our silence and I spoke with Adam once for a few minutes. He'd had a wonderful experience, he said, but now he was anxious to drive back to Los Angeles to be with his wife. I wished him a happy New Year. I drove back to San Francisco, singing, glad to be alive.

A great secret lies at the heart of every experience of suffering, and I believe anyone who is steadfast enough can find it. It's not much of a secret really, because the great spiritual teachers have been proclaiming it from the rooftops for thousands of years, but few of us find it because we spend most of our time running from our suffering. The spiritual path requires that we stand still, stop running, and face pain with courage and openness. Anyone who goes to the core of his or her longing, grief, loneliness, and anguish finds something that can never be touched by any suffering. Our troubles are like a tunnel: if we go all the way through them, we emerge into the sunlight. The depth of our deepest pain sinks hardly an inch into the ocean of being, but the ocean is fathomless. No one who has ever explored those depths has found any limit to the love, the peace, and the bliss in the depths of being. But this truth requires work and discipline to realize. If Adam had shown any interest in me during the retreat, I would have broken my commitments and become involved with him in a second. Yet that would have been a net loss. The deepest spiritual truths only reveal themselves when we take time to be alone with ourselves, to stop striving for a while, and to become still.

One of my fears as I traveled farther down my spiritual path was that my growth would completely alienate me from other gay men and the gay community. In fact, the reverse has been the case. I work as a psychotherapist with a primarily gay male clientele, and when I began incorporating mindfulness practices and spirituality into my therapy, the work was completely revitalized. I also began to experiment with offering public workshops for gay men on such themes as "Sexuality and Spirituality" and "Spiritual Practices for Opening the Heart." Every workshop I offered filled up almost immediately, and there were requests that they be repeated. It seems that the farther I progress in my own spiritual journey, the more gay men I find who are walking the same path.

"Groveling man knows well," wrote Paramahansa Yogananda, "Despair is seldom alien. Yet these are perversities, no true part of a man's true lot. The day he wills, his feet are set on the path to freedom."[1] It is true. The moment I seriously said, "There must be a better way! There must be a life that is richer and more fulfilling than this one!" the way to that deeper life opened to me.

I sometimes hear young gay men say, "Die young and leave a beautiful corpse!" But this is the voice of cynicism, despair, and fear. To my younger brothers, I say: Let yourself receive the gifts of every stage in life, and die old, in the incomparable beauty of your spirit.

NOTE

1. Paramahansa Yogananda (1972). *Autobiography of a Yogi* (p. 496). Los Angeles: Self-Realization Fellowship.

Chapter 3

Breaking Through

Alan L. Ellis

He knew now that a more comprehensive view of the world was to be had from physical depression than from intelligence.

Yukio Mishima, *The Decay of the Angel*[1]

When I was about eight years of age, I was told that a woman down the street claimed to talk to the dead. Having grown up in a religious community, I wasn't surprised by such claims. However, shortly after learning of her visitations from departed souls, I was told that she had a mental collapse. I asked my father and some other adults about this thing that everyone was quietly referring to as a "nervous breakdown." The term confused and frightened me. I first envisioned it literally although that made little sense—I couldn't imagine nerves breaking down. None of the adults was able to give me a satisfactory answer, and not being able to understand it led me to fear it even more. Some thirty years later, I found out that my mother had gone through a breakdown immediately following my birth—she experienced a severe postpartum depression that lasted nearly two years. My family, not unlike many families, had a strong, largely unconscious commitment to denial, and my finding out about my mother's breakdown some thirty-eight years after it occurred leaves little doubt about that commitment. We actively—if not somewhat unconsciously—avoided dealing directly with uncomfortable emotions and events and sought to maintain a constant, seemingly safe, but completely flat emotional state.

Because of her psychological condition, my mother was unable to attend to me. She has told me that I was largely ignored during the first two years of my life. She says that my father, who was so thrilled with the arrival of my older brother—who was born after twelve years of marriage in which it appeared my parents could not conceive a child—couldn't or wouldn't relate to me. She even says that my father's behavior toward me was so unusual that his own mother was surprised and disturbed by it. Thirty years later—following their divorce and my coming out—my mother wrote a pamphlet in which she argued that my father's behavior toward me created an unresolved need for male companionship that resulted in my being gay. Unfortunately, her focus on finding an explanation is based on an underlying belief that being gay is a problem in need of resolution. My father died a few years ago. My mother continues to hope for the day that I ultimately marry a woman and fulfill *her* dreams—dreams that are tied to my mother's strong commitment to and belief in her church. In an effort to be the best little boy in the world (to make up for early awareness of my "deficiency"), I had hoped to realize those dreams. The reality of my life, and especially my sexuality, required that I let go of those dreams. Even so, those dreams were strongly ingrained in my childhood psyche. Those dreams required that I be straight and I tried—I even went through aversion therapy when I was twenty-five. No one who knows anything about the lack of efficacy of such therapy would be surprised at its failure in my case.

While success as a heterosexual was not possible, I did succeed in the other aspects of my life—at least through my mid-thirties. I completed my bachelor's degree in accounting in two and a half years, graduating *summa cum laude* from one of the best programs in the country. I then traveled around the world as an auditor and later went on to get a PhD and a faculty position in social psychology. I authored academic articles and books and succeeded in my career. Only recently did I begin to understand that much of the motivation behind my efforts to succeed came from a desire to make up for the one area in which I had failed—to one day wake up and be attracted to women.

I now realize that, after I came out fifteen years ago, I feared that failure would mean that my sexuality was bad.

* * *

In 1992, I left a faculty position in the psychology department at the University of Kentucky to move to San Francisco. For four years, I feared that by living in Kentucky I was missing out on a "real life." I also needed to confront my own homophobia. Although I was out to my colleagues and the graduate students in Kentucky, I was only "out" intellectually. They knew I was gay, but I only once introduced them to someone I was dating. I could provide them with the "concept" of a gay person but not the reality of one. Fearing that my own internalized homophobia would never be resolved in a conservative place such as Lexington, I gave up my tenure-track position and moved to San Francisco.

Financially, the move was a challenge, and for years I barely made enough to support myself. However, I was working on a book about gay issues in the workplace—a book that I had dreamed of writing since coming out. I also had periodic work at a center that offered psychosocial support to people with life-challenging illnesses. With that job, I spent several months working at similar centers in Zagreb, Croatia, Guadalajara, Mexico, and Moscow. I was in my midthirties and felt that my life—while not perfect—could at least be perceived as interesting. The important thing was that it be perceived as a good life. As long as people believed that mine was a good life, a successful life, I would not have to confront the distorted connection that I had made between success and my sexuality. So I worked very hard to create the perception that my life "worked." It was only years later that I realized how much of my energy went into creating that impression rather than into what I was actually doing with my life. What others thought of me was extremely critical to the construction of my identity, to its very existence. Underlying that was my belief that it was extremely important to justifying my sexuality—as long as I was successful, my homosexuality would be okay.

In 1995, the grants and other funding sources for my position at the center ended. I was teaching a couple of courses at San Francisco State University as an adjunct professor, and had two books scheduled for publication. The publisher expected the book on gay issues in the workplace to do well—I expected to be able to continue to support myself without getting a full-time job. I was somewhat anxious after having spent three years without a steady job but I was able to mask the anxiety by continuing to believe that I would someday realize my new dreams—dreams that included writing books on gay issues, establishing a network of friends, and finding a significant other.

Over the next six months, however, I grew more anxious as I began to realize that the book was not going to sell that well. Although the book did well compared to others on the same topic, corporations were not interested in spending much money to include queer people as part of the diversity mix. I would soon be broke. I found evidences of failure everywhere—I was thirty-eight, had no money, no job, and had lost hope that my expectations and dreams would ever materialize. I began to berate myself for what I then saw as having believed in some grand illusion of who I was or could be. I began to obsess about being a failure. I even used the fact that I had a PhD to further support my self-denigration and hatred—other people with graduate degrees had certainly done better than I. I had pursued some foolish dream that was also intricately tied to my sexuality and I had failed. I felt as though mere common sense would have prevented the circumstances that I then found myself in and that nagging, painful belief that my sexuality was bad and that I would suffer for it was only reinforced by how I perceived my situation. While I could come up with a variety of reasons for why I felt I had failed, the one that was foremost was because I had pursued my homosexuality. I feared that the homophobes and the fundamentalists would be shown to be right.

* * *

Throughout my life, others have perceived me as extremely calm—as a calming influence. I remember in my early twenties giving a talk before which I literally thought I would die from the nervousness and anxiety that I felt. Following the talk, several people came up and said that they wished that they could be so calm and articulate when speaking before a large group. Only recently have I considered the possibility of a connection between this need to appear calm and my sexuality. My need to appear calm was based on the need to hide any internal anxiety. It seems highly probable that this behavior has its roots in my fear of being "found out," of others knowing that I was attracted to men, not women. At age fourteen, I remember being in a group of my peers as they made fun of queers, faggots, and butt-packers. I feared that if anyone asked me to speak, they would know I was one because my throat was so constricted from the terror that I would have been unable to respond. I struggled with all my might to keep from trembling, to sit calmly, to not give myself away.

After that experience, I did everything in my power to appear calm and to control any anxiety. If I could do so under a variety of circumstances, I would be able to protect my horrible secret—there would be no trembling voice or other manifestation of anxiety that would tell the world who I was. Even after I came out, I continued to maintain a tight rein on any anxiety I felt. For example, the time I spent in Moscow was one of the darkest periods of my life. The chaos of a system largely failing to make the transition to democracy had led to a *five-year decrease* in the life expectancy for males in just five years. A palpable sense of despair throughout the city matched my internal state at the time. Yet others did not see it. In fact, their perceptions of me were completely the opposite. At the end of my three weeks in Moscow, the volunteers and staff of the center spoke about how calm I was—several even expressed the hope that they some day could be so calm and centered. The staff in Zagreb had said the same thing. Little had changed since that talk in my early twenties or that moment in my teens. In Moscow, however, I finally acknowledged that the disconnect between what was going on psychologically and emotionally for me and how others perceived me based on my external behavior was total and complete.

The breakdown itself came a year after my return from Moscow. Six months prior to the breakdown, after realizing that the book sales would not support me, I found contract work as a technical writer. It paid relatively well, but I had a very difficult time making the transition from my identity as a college professor and author to that of a corporate writer. Although I didn't realize it at the time, having to give up the higher-status position of professor for a writing job brought me closer to feeling that I was a failure. That perception of failure made me increasingly anxious. Eventually, the anxiety became so acute that I could no longer work. All of my emotional resources collapsed—nothing was left to combat the fear that I had failed, let alone to carry on the demands of a job. On July 1, 1996, I went into work and told the owners that I had to leave and that I didn't know when I would return. It would be two months before I returned to work.

At the time, I was also teaching two summer courses at San Francisco State, and I felt an obligation to continue to teach those two courses as they had already begun. Although I had previously found the classroom to be a satisfying and fulfilling experience, I found it excruciatingly difficult to complete the remaining six weeks. I would spend the hour before either course began breathing deeply in an effort to lower the anxiety and terror that then pervaded my life. I could then just barely make it through the class.

Up to that point in my life, I had always found refuge in the deepest recesses of my mind—there I could escape from the world outside, a world that often frightened me. Although I had learned to be fairly successful in social settings, I would take whatever moments I could to withdraw psychologically to replenish my resources. But at the time of the breakdown, it was in those very recesses of the mind where the terror lay. I found no solace there, only fear—fear that I would never be able to function as a competent adult again. The terror sapped every ounce of my emotional and psychological energy. My only desire during that period was to be unconscious—all conscious distractions failed or else fueled the anxiety.

Ironically, at least on the surface, the external circumstances of my life appeared to be good—I was dating a guy who had a three-acre estate near Monterey with a swimming pool that could have come straight out of a 1930s' movie scene. We went to dinners in Santa Cruz and spent nights camping at Big Sur. Also, I had just published two books and in the past eighteen months, had traveled around the world. Had the terror not been so overwhelming, I could easily have continued to create the illusion that my life was okay. But nothing external mattered anymore.

Not even the parties helped—the parties that were exactly the "real life" that I feared I was missing out on when I lived in Kentucky. The parties were held around the pool and were hosted by members of "Barely Social," a group that met and socialized in the nude. The lack of clothing led to a lack of pretense, which under different circumstances I would have enjoyed. Instead, whenever anyone talked about their work or some other purposeful activity, a piercing terror would run through me. It didn't matter that my job was waiting for me—I feared I would never be able to support myself again or to function like a normal person. Although there may have been no rational basis for that fear, it was clear to me that the terror was not rational either. As long as I was in the grip of that terror, I could not work. Every aspect of life felt like a tremendous burden—the simplest activities of life wore me out and overwhelmed me.

One morning after spending the night in terror in my apartment in the city, I went to my doctor's office as soon as it opened—I showed up without an appointment. I was given a prescription for an anti-anxiety drug and a referral to a psychiatrist. I returned to my boy-friend's house near Monterey and was able to experience about an hour of relief by taking two of the pills. I would sit on a couch and rock back and forth—staring at a bougainvillea plant overhanging one of the windows. I tried to maintain a state of stupor, to not think about anything because anxiety permeated every thought. Then, as the effects of the drug wore off, the questions surrounding what I was going to do would return and the anxiety would escalate.

I had an appointment with the psychiatrist in five days. Five days seemed like an eternity—I didn't think I could make it through five more days, so I started taking my boyfriend's Prozac. I began with a full dose (a serious mistake, as one should start out with a small dose and work up gradually to the standard dose). Rather than calming the anxiety, the Prozac caused it to increase significantly—I couldn't believe that it could be any worse. For the next five days, I was unable to fully compre-hend my experience—life became a haze in which I could only process a limited amount of what was happening around me.

With the psychiatrist's help, I found an antidepressant that worked for me. It numbed the terror and facilitated a period of great internal change. The way my mind operated seemed to change. Whereas I had previously been shy and overly concerned about what others thought, I now become somewhat extroverted and much less concerned about what anyone else thought of my behavior or actions. I began to realize that previously, the vast majority of my energy had been spent obsess-ing about what I had just said or about what others would think of what I was doing. It was a tremendous waste of energy that left me with very little stamina to accomplish anything. The medication helped free this energy so that it could be applied to what I was doing rather than to interpreting what others might think. It was as if a tremendous surge of energy had been given to me. The medication also allowed me to "watch" my thoughts—it eliminated the anxiety, which freed me to just observe what I was thinking. Thoughts that previously produced anxiety would appear but then leave—it was as if the anxiety was the fuel that maintained the obsession with those thoughts. Without the anxiety, those thoughts passed through like any other thoughts.

I've heard that Carl Jung, in the latter years of his life, refused to offer therapy to anyone under the age of thirty-five. His reasoning was that up to that age, people were too busy constructing their identities to really analyze the identity that they had created. I suspect that the source of the midlife crisis is the moment that we seriously begin to analyze the identity that we've created. I also suspect that that process forces us to confront our unmet expectations and to reevaluate the origins of those expectations. The antidepressant allowed me to engage in that analysis and examination.

My analysis led me to mourn and let go of my failure to meet a number of long-held expectations—many of which belonged to someone or something outside myself. I had internalized a surprising number of expectations, not because I really wanted them, but because I had hoped to satisfy someone else's expectations for my life—to justify my sexuality.

I also had to mourn the loss of a number of expectations that I valued. Part of growing older is realizing that I will not be able to do everything I had imagined or hoped to accomplish. My analysis has also led to an awareness of the tenacity of some of my less-desired personality traits—traits that I hoped would have corrected themselves by now. At some level, what I need to do is more fully accept those aspects of my self—I guess that is what is referred to as integrating one's shadow.

There are still plenty of shadows and moments of despair and sadness, and the terror comes and goes. Some say that the terror is a guide. Clearly, the preceding years of terror and its occasional waning helped me to let go of or at least recognize a number of beliefs and expectations that were harming me. As a result, I feel less burdened and more of my energy is now available for what I wish to accomplish. The terror also forced me to be more conscious of the effect that earlier events in my life had on me and now—to a degree—I can chose whether or not to let them continue to influence me.

In discussing the past several years with a friend who is both a therapist and a shaman, I was encouraged to consider my experience a breakthrough rather than a breakdown—a helpful distinction and, ultimately, an accurate one. Although my process of breaking through is not over and clearly will not end in this lifetime, I do feel that my focus is now on recognizing, working through, and learning from my fears rather than attempting to ban them from consciousness.

Fifteen years ago when I was first coming out, I repeatedly asked my closest friend (who was straight) why I was gay. I quit asking the question when he responded with "Well, who better than you?" In a better world, that would be the question directed to every gay teenager. For me, the second half of my life is an opportunity to more fully realize the truth of that statement.

NOTE

1. Mishima, Y. (1974). *The Decay of the Angel* (p. 213). Translated from the Japanese by Edward G. Seidensticker. Tokyo: Charles E. Tuttle Company.

Chapter 4

I'm Still Here

Stephen W. Goodin

It was March 1983. I had just seen the doctor again about my swollen lymph nodes. I was trying to ignore them, but my partner had insisted that I originally see the doctor, so now I was visiting regularly. Michael had pushed me to go, saying, "Stephen, there's something wrong" every time he touched my throat. No one knew then that this was a symptom of AIDS, not even the doctor. We simply called it gay lymph node syndrome.

I was twenty-three and had just started my career in computers. I was a mainframe operator at a data-processing center with offices on the wharf in San Francisco. It was a killer job with a high-profile company that offered great benefits. I even had parking privileges.

After this latest visit, the doctor sent my blood to a blind antibody study conducted at UCSF. The results indicated a virus, and he wanted me to confirm this finding with the new test that the health department offered. This test also came back positive. I was devastated. Immediately after being told, I was sent to a room to meet with a counselor, who asked me how I thought I was going to deal with the results. I was extremely emotional, tearing up, and fearful. All I knew was that this virus killed people. The counselor suggested that I consider going to a support group and gave me Project Inform's number.

For a year, the lymph nodes stayed the same, but no other signs of illness or disease occurred. Then, suddenly, my blood work changed. I had lost all my platelets. For the first time, I actually realized that this sickness was inside me. To cope, I decided to join a support group. Most members of the support group were taking AZT, and I learned how AZT affected them. The effects of the AZT seemed as debilitating as the disease itself. I decided to stay drug free. I cry as I think of so many people using AZT in pain, and then dying. Others were trying all sorts of treatments in desperate attempts to survive this disease.

I continued to appear and feel healthy. I also felt motivated by my career. After two years at the job on the wharf, I applied for another position. Shortly thereafter, I was offered a job with a multinational gas company that required taking a health exam for employment. I drove myself crazy wondering if they would discover my secret. Rumors circulated about how the disease was the work of the government and Ronald Reagan—that it had been created to eliminate gays. I feared that the first impact would be that I wouldn't get this job. Nothing showed up in the health report, so I started work.

Because of the drop in my platelet count, my doctor referred me to a hematologist, who never made eye contact with me. He said that my spleen was consuming my platelets and that I needed to have it removed. The diagnosis was idiopathic thrombocytopenic purpura (ITP). All I could think about was that they wanted to cut me open. Yet nobody really seemed to know what the hell was going on, so I decided I would live with my body whole and keep going. I decided not to have the operation to remove my spleen. Surprisingly, my doctor supported this decision. The support group was less enthusiastic. One person in the group had had his spleen removed and he believed the operation made him better. In a rather heated discussion, I became angry and said that the medical world didn't know enough about this virus and consequently all of our friends are glowing with AZT or getting cut up. Several in the group were taking AZT. I said that if I had to kill myself I would do so before I would use that drug. Not surprisingly, this upset several members of the group. I felt that many had turned their lives over to their doctors; they wanted to be told what to do. I often thought that they wouldn't know if they had a runny nose unless their doctor told them about it.

I believed that the doctor needed to be my partner and to discuss things with me. My father was a pharmacist and my mother was a hematologist, so I grew up asking medical questions. As a result, I made my own decisions regarding my therapy—I did not simply go along with the latest trend.

My spleen stayed in my body. The platelet count remained low, but I had no additional symptoms. In lieu of the operation, I decided to learn how to fly. I got my pilot's license over the next year.

I also joined a study group for gay men with ITP at UCSF. Inga, the nurse practitioner, was doing a study on how visualization and energy work affected the virus. In the visualizations, we took deep breaths and imagined a beautiful place. We visualized the sun shining and then turning into a warm orange liquid that entered our bodies and purified them. We also imagined battles with men running across fields and engaging the virus, or laser guns attacking it. Inga also would move her hands within close proximity of our bodies and "flick" the negative energy to the sides. Many years later, I would see some members of the group who were still leading healthy lives.

During this time, I was grateful to know that my partner did not have the virus. However, the virus was affecting our relationship, as my sex drive had shut down. I couldn't live with the thought that I might give the virus to someone, thus it was very difficult for me to be intimate or to have sex with anyone. Very rarely, I would get drunk and have sex, usually with anonymous partners and always as safely as possible. But for the most part, my sex life was nonexistent.

At the same time, Michael and I and another gay couple moved to the suburbs near my work. I felt as if we were in a fishbowl being observed by the neighbors who seemed to be wondering what the four men in that house were doing and who they were.

As I learned more about HIV, I began to think less and less about the future. Certainly IRAs and retirement planning were not on the agenda. Decisions were short term. I focused primarily on how to avoid being dependent on my stepparents, friends, the state, or an AIDS hospice.

I had a number of friends with whom I had shared my health status. These confidants—David, Bill, Murray, Scott, Carl, Ken, and many others—are all gone now. Some of them hadn't shared that they too were ill; I think they just wanted to deny that it was happening.

Time continued to pass; people continued to die. Inside, I was coming apart but on the outside, I appeared to be a successful young man. In 1985, we moved back to Oakland where I took a different job for two years. Then I accepted another job in San Francisco that included a large raise as well as recognition of my skills.

I acquired a new set of friends in the city, and found greater access to information about HIV. I also joined a new support group. I was constantly wondering how long it would be before I died.

The crowd in the city eased me back into leading a relatively normal life. I would go out, have a few drinks on occasion, dance in my briefs at the End Up. It was five years since I was first diagnosed. Michael and I were still living together, but no longer as a couple. I wasn't dating, and even though I was attracted to many men my fear would not allow a close relationship. So I worked hard and got top ratings at work. I also traveled a lot.

Then my boss and mentor at my job died of AIDS.

I was very worried. Friends were dying, and the drugs were not working for anyone. I refused to use them even though my doctor would often encourage me to start AZT monotherapy. I said, "You guys don't know what you're doing so I'm not going to take it."

Instead, I took vitamins. I followed Dr. Jon Kaiser's nutrition program. (Kaiser is the author of several books including *Healing HIV: How to Rebuild Your Immune System.*) I did what made sense to me, and I continued to do visualizations. If nothing else, the visualizations helped relieve my stress and also helped me to feel that I was in control. I believed any decisions regarding my health were up to me because the medical community clearly did not know enough about the virus or how to control it.

In 1988, my feelings for Michael became even more distant and our relationship continued to deteriorate. I think I just wanted change but couldn't summon the courage to try to make it. Although I felt very confident about my work, my self-confidence concerning my personal life dropped. I looked fine, but many of my friends didn't and I could only wonder when I would begin to look like them. I did try dating other HIV-positive men, as I felt more comfortable with them because of our common experience. However, I couldn't seem to find a companion who was serious about taking care of himself. The men I met seemed to want to party to the grave. Many had already given up. This attitude almost made me feel as if I was wrong. What good were vitamins? Nevertheless, I didn't quit.

From 1983 to 1989, all I thought about was, "What am I going to do?" It wasn't really about terror or shock; it was more a question to determine what was happening. Every day someone died, a new disease surfaced, or there was some new symptom or problem associated with the virus. I felt as if I had a glass beaker around my neck that could break any day, and then life would be over.

By 1989, the medical community appeared to have the virus and its manifestations pretty well nailed. They just didn't have a cure. Time continued to pass and I was still alive. In October 1989, the Loma Prieta earthquake hit. I had made arrangements to leave work early that day to watch the World Series between Oakland and San Francisco on television, but at the last minute my boss insisted that I stay. I was upset but realized later that I would have been on the Bay Bridge when the quake hit had I not stayed at work. The quake made me question whether I wanted to continue to live in Oakland. What would happen in such an urban area during a huge disaster?

In 1990, I woke up early one morning around 3:00 a.m. and couldn't move. I felt as if I had been hit by a car. It took five or six minutes to get my bearings. I finally managed to roll off the bed, get to the shower, and create some steam that helped me breathe. I called a neighbor who drove me across the Bay Bridge to the hospital. It was terrifying riding across that bridge in the dark, looking at the bright lights of the city and wondering what was happening to me. I ended up stuck in a cold wheelchair for an hour in the emergency room, angry and waiting for attention. Finally, a doctor examined me, prescribed some pills, and sent me home. I had nonspecific pneumonia, not pneumocystis, and it cleared up in two days. Nevertheless, it was a big scare.

In 1991, I bought a BMW K (1000) bike and started driving around the western United States. I had had bikes when I was younger, but gave them up when I began to worry about hurting myself. I feared that any procedures resulting from an accident would cause my immune system to drop. I began to avoid taking risks. I was even somewhat paranoid about getting viruses from others or having any sort of contact that might hurt me. My T-cell count was dropping, but I decided that I must LIVE NOW. It had been eight years since I was diagnosed with the virus and I was still alive, so I decided to take care of myself but also to do what I enjoyed. I was thirty-two.

I still had moments of weakness when friends died or the news from the doctor was bad, but I maintained a positive attitude. I was doing well and was asymptomatic. I did get flak from some members of my support group. One even yelled at me saying, "You're so fucking positive. Doesn't anything bad ever happen to you?" I wasn't denying the bad stuff, but I didn't feel as if I was "decaying."

Almost everyone I met at the time was HIV positive. That helped me realize just how big this disease was. At least I wasn't alone.

I moved on to another job for a company that was a pioneer in developing wide area networks. I had a lot of knowledge about token rings and IBM technology, and I was good at what I did. I had the opportunity to go to Europe for the company and I took it. I was afraid to go because of the disease, but I went. Over the next couple of years, I traveled to Mexico, Hawaii, and Amsterdam.

In 1992, I took a job in Marin County that offered long-term disability, life insurance, and good health benefits. My general health was deteriorating, and the pneumonia had scared me into thinking that I should not just keep jumping around. My T-cell count was still dropping and the doctor again urged me to go on AZT monotherapy. I was getting tired; my endurance was diminishing. My body was clearly changing and I couldn't tell if it was due to age or the virus.

I still kept busy. I went skiing in the winter and camping in the summer. I went dancing at the clubs because I didn't want to be alone, forced to think about what was happening to my body. I worked graveyard and afternoon shifts in the computer room. I did whatever I could to keep busy by working and traveling. I earned a good salary and had enough money to keep myself away from home.

Thrush and other opportunistic infections began to occur. I lost weight and became fatigued. I did start taking the AZT, but couldn't tolerate it so I switched to D4T. As my health deteriorated, I became less social and more withdrawn. Why form friendships if I was just going to die? Work was fine, except that I would sometimes fall asleep at my desk. My self-confidence outside of work was very low. I talked about suicide. I didn't want to be in a hospital bed.

In late 1994, I revealed my health status to my boss. We talked about my retiring, but I didn't want to abandon my career because to me that meant that the end was near. Quitting meant that the virus was winning. This decision was incredibly painful. I told my parents that I was retiring; they told me that they were very proud of me. I told others and then I began to arrange my private affairs. I put together my will, made burial plans, put everything in order.

In June 1995, I rode my bicycle in the AIDS ride from San Francisco to Los Angeles. I was amazed that I was able to do it, but when I came home I immediately went into the hospital. I was having terrible problems with the thrush, but an endoscopy found nothing. My T-cell count was below 100, my days were very short, and my weight continued to drop. I started taking both D4T and AZT, and I felt a little better.

I spent the last two months of 1995 in South Africa, with a motorcyclist friend who had returned to Cape Town where he had grown up. He had parties; his mother had been a former mayor of Cape Town and he knew a lot of people. The trip was very hard on me because I started feeling physically worse, but I was hesitant to seek medical attention there. I spent a lot of money buying anything I wanted and doing as I pleased.

I spent New Year's Eve at a bar in Cape Town, looking over the street from a balcony and wondering whether I'd see the end of the new year. I had just lost the ability to masturbate; my body was shutting down. I was getting weaker and weaker. I arrived in Cape Town weighing 160 pounds. I left weighing 140 pounds.

A few days later, I packed my clothes and headed home. I could only stay awake three or four hours a day. I took numerous pills. My T-cell count fell to 23, but I still did not have any opportunistic infections. I had trouble with thrush and diarrhea, though.

In April 1996, the new drugs arrived—the protease inhibitors. My doctor gave me the pills, and I took the goddamn things. I felt an overwhelming mix of chemicals in my body. I could taste them in my saliva. I threw up all the time. The side effects were very severe. A week later, I told the doctor that I was considering stopping everything and killing myself. He grabbed me and said, "Give it one more week." He asked me to promise him that, saying that I could then stop taking the drugs if I couldn't handle the effects.

I went home and started looking for viatical settlement companies. I had decided that I was going to party to my death. But for a week, I took the pills. It was horrible. I was incontinent all the time. I wondered why I was alive and I wanted to die.

The following week, the blood work showed that the drugs had had a significant effect on my viral load. It had dropped a great deal. My T-cell count had doubled to 46. The doctor told me these were great results. A ray of hope came out of the darkness, and I continued to take the pills. Even so, 1996 was the worst year of my life. I felt terrible every day, and thought about killing myself every one of those days.

I did manage to ride my motorcycle as crew for the AIDS ride that year. I could only do a half-day shift. I told everyone it would be my last ride.

When I returned, I had a letter saying that the viatical settlement had gone through. There was $180,000 in my account.

I took a camping trip with friends to Alaska. I rode my bike to Seattle where I caught a ferry to Alaska. My friends drove a camper and I followed them around, following the kitchen, so to speak. It was July and the weather was warm and the scenery was beautiful.

When I returned, I decided to leave the apartment in Oakland and to leave Michael. I didn't want to die in that apartment or in my parents' spare bedroom. So to protect myself, I decided to buy a house in the Redwoods where I knew others with HIV lived.

I found a house and moved my stuff there by myself. Michael didn't support the move. He told me we might never talk again and that I was making the wrong decision. At the time, I didn't care what kind of damage I was doing because I felt that no one could know what I was going through. I pushed people away.

I moved to the house to die. A nice, safe, pretty, quiet place in a rural setting. I didn't want to be weak and vulnerable in the city. I had seen older women attacked outside our apartment building—hit on the head and robbed. I wanted control as well. I had first looked at some apartments and got the feeling that I wasn't welcome because I had AIDS. I was worn out and my attitude was "Fuck you and leave me alone—I'm dying, and you bastards don't have any idea what I'm going through." But then I'd pick up a motorcycle or skiing magazine and have a moment where I envisioned something I liked doing.

I arranged my finances so that I would always be able to cover the mortgage and food. It was September 1996. The town flooded that winter. My house was above the flood and in it I kept getting better.

The drugs were terrible, though. I could be dressed up, standing in Macy's, and suddenly I would lose control of my bowels. I remember being stuck in traffic and frantically grabbing for the rear floor mat so that I could prevent staining the car upholstery. But as of June 1996, my viral load was and has remained undetectable.

I spent 1997 getting better, kicking back, meeting others who were retired on disability, and hanging out at the pool at a local resort. I enjoyed the summer of 1997, and my hopes were rising. People even expressed a sexual attraction to me. I resumed dating that summer but I still had difficulty performing sexually. It was very discouraging, but I came to understand that this is a common side effect of the medication.

As the year passed, I grew restless and bored. I considered going back to work part-time. I could work up to twenty hours per week and not lose my disability. So on January 1, 1998, I returned to work for the same company I had left three years earlier.

I had expected to die, but now I was recovering. I was afraid that the recovery was not for real. I did a lot of research before going back to work to ensure that I wouldn't lose my Social Security or disability—just in case.

In June 1998, I went back to Europe for a motorcycle trip. I met my friend from Cape Town, Brian, in Munich and we traveled around on our bikes. He said that I looked great. For me, the light had changed from red to green and I had permission to go ahead with life. Brian had been there when the light had turned to what I thought was a permanent red.

During the trip, the logistics of the drugs made travel challenging. One required refrigeration, and so I had to take an ice chest to Europe. I also had to eat at specific times of the day. It was difficult, but I made it work.

By the end of 1998, the effects of the drugs stabilized. My body now tolerates the drugs without the horrible side effects of the first three years. I still experience flash diarrhea, but I know when it's happening. It's no longer a surprise.

Despite everything, I still have a positive attitude. I also used common sense to take care of myself. The question before me now is how do I learn to trust life again now that I have scratched and clawed my way to forty? On my thirtieth birthday, I wondered if I would make it to thirty-five.

Five years ago, I was somewhat cynical about my life. I felt my fate was sealed and I tried to plan for it. I thought fate had decreed my death, but instead I lived. The moral of the story is that anything can happen. It's so easy to fuck your life up worrying too much about things that may or may not happen.

I still feel survivor guilt.

Throughout the many years of HIV-positive gay men trying Compound Q, DMSO, having their blood pumped out, heated up, and then pumped back in, it was always clear to me that the medical establishment was stabbing in the dark. I decided to wait, to visualize, and to let my body fight the fight until I thought it could no longer do so.

I always tried to go with my feelings. Now I want to learn to trust again. All those years are like the end of a love affair—something that you were intimately close to but don't want to experience again.

Right now, my brain is challenged again. I love my work. I just took a full-time position that pays a six-figure salary. The conditions of my life now make me feel as though I am living a different reality, far removed from that which I lived so recently. I now face questions I had long ago dismissed as irrelevant. For example, should I plan for retirement? So rather than confronting my own death, I'm confronting the challenges of life because, much to my surprise, I'm still here.

Chapter 5

Before a (Prospective) Visit to the Land of the Lotus Eaters

Alejandro Medina-Bermúdez

Let us alone, What is it that will last?
All things are taken from us, and become
Portions and parcels of the dreadful Past.

Alfred, Lord Tennyson, The Lotos-Eaters

A gay man in his middle years. I have been asked to write on being a gay man in his middle years.

In my middle years, that is.

I am forty-seven years old, and I could have been a baby boomer: one of those baby boomers in praise of whom a book of poems has been published recently by a group of female baby boomers. I heard about the book on *NPR* while driving from Chicago to Peoria. Some of the poems were read out loud over the radio and I liked them. As expressed in common parlance, I was able to "relate" to them.

Yes, I could have been a baby boomer: I, too, while growing up, sat often in front of a black-and-white television screen which flashed hypnotically its daily pensum of images, like an open window onto the improbable lives of women who always appeared as beautiful/repellent and bitchy/pitiful as Bette Davis or Joan Crawford, crying on the shoulders of men as ugly/handsome and bastard/heroic as Humphrey Bogart or Clark Gable. I, too, occasionally, listened to the romantic cooings of Paul Anka or danced to the electrifying cat calls of Elvis Presley. And as a child growing up, I, too, used to ride inside a blue Chevrolet while I watched my father shift gears three consecutive times, after which I would sit back, snuggly at his side, and let the exhilarating sensation of increasing speed pull my body down into the seat, every time to my recovered amazement and his repeated amusement.

All of the above would have given me the right to qualify as a baby boomer. Except that "baby boomer" is a thoroughly postwar, middle-class American concept, and I was born, yes, inside a middle-class family, but in Cuba, not in the United States, son to a father who once managed to escape the gory massacre of the Spanish Civil War—my father had fought against Franco, and had been a soldier in the Madrid Front. My mother was the second youngest of seven children raised by well-established provincials who, in turn, were the offspring of Italian and Canary Island immigrants: my Italianate grandmother kept the house while my *Isleño* grandfather kept a shop. That was all back in a small city which basked in the tropical sun of the deep Cuban country-side like a drowsy body napping exposed on the grass in the middle of an endless plain—not Montana-like endless, mind you, just regular human-size endless: a flat, round horizon, which to the child that I was then did seem to embrace all dreams in one big, sun-drenched hug, to an endless plain made exclusively for a child's imagination, where clouds as large as ships sailed across the lilac skies and heads of cattle could be counted individually as they grazed gently on either side of the road while father and I drove in the blue Chevrolet across the land, the *fincas*—closer to the lazy Mediterranean *cortijos* of southern Spain than to the efficient puritanical farms of the American Midwest—glistening with flashes of hot color at the end of pastures meant for cows instead of sugar cane or tobacco.

But I am straying from my subject, which is the story of a gay man in my middle years. I suppose I started on my past history because, as with any story, background is context, and context creates a semblance of understanding. But I also suspect that, if my thoughts move first and automatically to my ethnic/national/linguistic memories when asked to talk about myself, then it is probably because, unlike a "true" American baby boomer, there are unresolved issues of identity at stake here which lay deep under the surface, deeper at any rate than my own sexuality, yet inextricably bound with it; issues which over-flow their container, both determining the structure of my "self " and at the same time savagely ingrown into it, like a bent toenail, hurting yet inseparable from the body against which it has turned.

Those issues are complex and varied. They start with a fundamental otherness, an *alienness*—when compared with baby boomer American experience—that must forever permeate my early memories and thus separates me from my American generational "counterparts." I remember listening to Paul Anka and to Elvis Presley, yes, but more than that, my musical memories (to give one specific example) refer to the *ur-salsero*, Beny Moré, also known as *"el bárbaro del ritmo,"* (when *salsa* was called many things but not that) and to *La Lupe*, the beautiful black woman with a throaty voice who sang sentimental *boleros* on television while beating her fists against the back of a defenseless pianist. (Almodóvar has been recovering her singing in his campiest—which is to say his best—films.) Equally pervasive was pop music from Continental Europe: the minimalist-melodic hits of Gigliola Cinquetti, for instance, or of Rita Pavone. There was also good Latin-American folk music: from the stentoreous macho bellowing of Mexican *rancheras*, laden with feminine sentimentality (gender roles are seldom what they seem in the Hispanic world, that world itself being, of course, as unhomogeneous as the full spectrum of world ethnicities and cultures), to the simmering passion of existential, angst-ridden Argentine *tangos*. And then, of course, we must not forget the usual staple of tasteless, glitzy Spanish *cupletistas* who paraded their festive tunes and clattering castanets around the island, their bodies abundantly clad in frilly polka-dot *sevillana* dresses, their heads and shoulders draped in delicate lace *mantillas,* their eyes and lips plastered with makeup, their necks and wrists covered with gold chains and dangling gold medals so that we Cubans might keep alive the umbilical cord to a mythical, innocuous Spanish past carefully selected, mummified, and exported by the watchful Kultural Kommisars of the Franco regime.

However, all that is trite stuff. I could not really begin to illustrate, much less define, my otherness to an American reader by piling up the examples, not even if I multiplied their number and ran a list as long as an encyclopedia.

More important is, it seems to me, that this "otherness" had to do with how a male child—in this case, myself—was brought up by the women in the family. (There was always more than one woman: at least one more, the grandmother; at times, there were also various sisters and aunts.) The bittersweet—indeed, *poisonous*—psychology of the otherwise masculine-driven middle-class white Cuban women of my mother's generation (I have already pointed out that gender roles seldom are what they seem in the multifaceted Hispanic world) has been well described, I think, by Lezama Lima in his alchemical (gay) literary masterpiece, *Paradiso*. That psychology permeated everything we children did and were: from our overcorrect social behavior and our carefully inculcated success-driven mentality to our impeccably starched-and-ironed school uniforms; from the sentimental poetry we used to learn by heart to the eau-de-cologne liberally splashed on the nape of our necks and the *gomina* lacquer unctuously, meticulously, combed into our hair in preparation for the afternoon walk through town with the family. Growing up middle class in Cuba during the 1950s meant, ultimately, becoming exercised in a particular—and very distinct from a North American—kind of physical touch and mating language; a touch and a language suffused with an infinite, secret, Mediterranean/Caribbean manly-feminine yearning that knew precisely how to mask itself publicly in order to be able to burn all the more passionately in the privacy of the bedroom.

On the other hand, coming of age in the United States as a gay adolescent (a gay adolescent whose past history, as I have already emphasized, differed substantially from that of other American adolescents, gay or not) also meant "coping"—another common parlance usage—with heart-tearing ideological issues. For the rest of the world (certainly for the progressive, prejudice-smashing Left), the Cuban "Revolution" meant the arrival of utopia on the American continent. Never mind that the endless stream of Cuban exiles—a mass exodus if there ever was one—contradicted all the pious wishes of that Left: the exiles were branded, after all, as "bad" Cubans, while the "good" ones were believed to be those who had remained behind, ready to put up a heroic fight rather than relinquish Humanity's dream of equality and justice finally come true in our little, beleaguered paradise island (not so little, though, nor so beleaguered: as big as Austria and Switzerland put together and backed by the full arsenal of the Soviet Union). But that same progressive Left that supported the Revolution worldwide also refused to hear about the mass executions, the political prisoners, the torture, and the terror. And of course, they turned their eyes away from the concentration camps purposely created for "undesirables," including, yes, gays. The book *Before Night Falls*, by Reinaldo Arenas, or the film *Improper Conduct*, by Néstor Almendros and Oscar Jiménez Leal, could have been damning, devastating testimonies; in fact, had they depicted similar horrors in any other part of the world, they *would* have become damning, devastating testimonies. But with Cuba things were different: in the name of ideology, a nasty, cruel, and demeaning dictatorship enjoyed endless supplies of universal good will, so that invariably, when the progressive Left looked at the island, heinous crimes were overlooked which for less civilized countries would have been considered unacceptable and would have raised world outrage. So it is that often I have been, and on occasions still am, confronted in gay publications with letters written by gay men and women justifying the political debacle in the island, lately citing with unmasked relief the film by *Titón* Gutiérrez Alea, *Fresa y chocolate,* as uncontestable proof that in recent times, life has improved for gays in the island (an unfalsified opinion which, by the way, indirectly negates earlier refusal to acknowledge that there had ever been anything wrong on the island at all). Those letters also applaud the apparent gains in freedom of speech (whereby these gay men and women have no clue about the humiliating, inquisitorial vigilance applied to the creation and distribution of *Titón*'s film or, for that matter, to the writing and publication of the short story—*El lobo, el bosque y el hombre nuevo,* by Senel Paz—on which it was based). On this point, understandably, the Cuban inside me who feels that he has been despoiled of his childhood, his home, and his identity and who cries out for justice in the name of other fellow humans, finds himself at grave odds with the gay community to which the gay in me—who defends freedom of lifestyles and the rights of gays openly to exist as contributing members in a sane and prosperous society—belongs.

Those two mutually contradictory tendencies have had the ultimate effect of canceling each other out for this would-have-been baby boomer, who grew up doing a precarious balancing act on a tightrope stretched in lieu of a bridge over the chasm opened between two worlds (Gustavo Pérez-Firmat, another Cuban-American intellectual, has aptly referred to the experience as "living on the hyphen"), the only way out of the impasse was to flee *all worlds*. Like Huckleberry Finn, I resent having gone through my own "sivilizing" process. Therefore, I escaped, the world having since become my own personal Mississippi River. First it was to France, right after college, where part of my father's family had lived after the Civil War. Then Germany. And finally so many other places that I have lost track.

Now I reside in Spain, but job, family, and culture bring me back to the United States several times a year. I am an American, and yet I am not one; or perhaps, again, the latter statement gives me away *particularly* as an American. But I identify more with a literary hero: Ulysses. Like him, I have died and been resurrected more than once, and I would like someday to rewrite the *Odyssey* as the tale of a journey—visit to Hades included—back from my own private Troy. (It matters not that others before me, from Virgil to Joyce, have exploited the myth, the greatness of classics being perhaps nothing other than their built-in capacity for reappropriation by every new generation of readers.)

Meanwhile, time keeps rushing forth like a river into a final waterfall, and a part of me watches motionless (and emotionless) as all my past resentments and discomforts (but also all my past joys and affirmations) recede into the foggy horizon at my back. I am, after all, a gay man in my middle years.

Artists in the Renaissance portrayed Time, *Chronos,* holding in his hand, like a fragile soap bubble, the twin inverted goblets of an hourglass, along with a sickle and the decrepitude of old age. Somehow those artists ended up conflating ancient images of *Chronos*, Time, with equally ancient ones of *Kronos,* Saturn, son of Uranus, the god who achieved independence by castrating his own father and then casting his father's genitals, Lorena Bobbitt-style, into the ocean, accidentally effecting that way the birth of Aphrodita Urania, motherless goddess of all beauty existing beyond the realm of the sensual. It seems like more and more often *Chronos/Kronos* sits saturnine and heavy before me. He watches in silence as he pushes toward me his hourglass, half filled—or half empty—with swiftly sliding sand, his menacing sickle threatening with castration, only this time without the promise of regeneration; the inevitable decay of my body in the not-so-far-off future and the menace of AIDS just behind my immediate past—Scylla and Charybdis—are watersheds that remind me that I must push on, on, toward the end, whatever that may be.

I wish I could give young gay men and women some words of wisdom, point to people I once knew and hold them up as role models; but all my old friends have died even as a new generation of boys and girls was springing forth; a generation which now shines as lovely as a wreath of young blossoms in the spring, colorful and beautiful and thoughtless as young blossoms always are, as they always have been, since the beginning of time, or at least since the beginning of our own history: since that day, for instance, when Socrates admired Charmides' perfect, fleeting nakedness in an Athenian gymnasium. It is too late for me to tell these youths anything, they who come too early for everything. No use speaking of the young messenger boy from the bread shop down the street who tried to seduce me at my piano teacher's house when I was barely eight, in Cuba; nor of my first true love in college, in the United States (oh his red-blond hair and the soft pink globes of his rump-cheeks!); he now lies under six feet of dirt. What do the young care that I saw the legalization of pornography in Paris, in the 1970s, or that at the end of that decade, *Pimpernel* was a hot gay disco in Cologne, Germany? It is a bitter truth, but ultimately perhaps an enlightening one, that each generation must discover the stuff of life anew, and that guidance is only recognized too late, generally arriving as a kind of poetic justice—the material from which great literature sometimes can be crafted—but not as the practical help it should have been when it was direly needed.

These days I feel like the invisible Narrator in *À la recherche du temps perdu* as he reaches the end of his unsought-for search and discovers that he is standing on his own past as if on two long, precarious stilts. Time stretches under him and he sways dangerously atop his own life, too far up for his own good and perhaps also for the good of others. After that discovery, nonetheless, the Narrator was finally able to go on and write his novel; Proust, on the other hand, was ready to die.

I am a gay man in his middle years. In my middle years, that is. I was born in Cuba forty-seven years ago, have lived many lives, many places, and don't really know who I am or where I belong. Maybe, like Ulysses, my name is *Oudéis:* Nobody. By the way, I am writing this inside a plane, in the middle of a flight, no longer sure whether I am coming or going, backward or forward over the Atlantic Ocean, toward a place that, for me in any case, will never again be Ithaca.

Ever.

Chapter 6

Waking Up on the Other Side

Kevin G. Barnhurst

A heart attack at age forty-three at least resolved one mystery. My health began declining when I moved three years before to Syracuse, New York. Sleeplessness, stomach pains, esophageal spasms—these baffled the physicians. They ruled out heart disease for want of any risk factors: six feet and 160 pounds since high school, low cholesterol and blood pressure, always active, no family history, and a low-stress teaching job. I felt debilitated, old, but the stomach tests all came back normal. Discomfort at middle age for me became routine.

It began a little after four, September 24, as I lay napping on the sofa. The pains seemed unremarkable—I'd felt them before. Richard, my partner of several years, snored undisturbed beside me. We'd spent the morning cleaning house: a quiet Sunday. Potent secrets enter my life that way, disguised in the mundane.

* * *

Growing up in Salt Lake City, I learned the usual ways for boys to fool with boys. Mike, a deacon from the old Fourth Ward, as they called our west side meeting house, first taught me to beat off. "You don't know?" he exclaimed as we walked home from Sunday school. My family rarely went to church, but I liked some Mormon revelations. Mike had two years' practice. He told me how to stroke, with a thumb and two fingers (he was bigger and could use his whole hand). The tingling starts in your toes, he said, and then builds up to your crotch, until you shoot in hot waves. I didn't ask what shot. He was making motions with one bronzed hand, then threw back his head, ecstatic. The sinews of his neck stood out. For one moment I could hardly breathe.

At home, it didn't work for me at first. Later my neighbor David invited me to his room. I still connect the smell of semen with his bed. He lived on the corner, in a nicer house with a console stereo, an immaculate mom, and a dad high up in the Mormon Church. I didn't love him but couldn't resist his room. I came there regularly until it started to hurt when I peed, and a doctor gave me penicillin but didn't explain why. David's older brother Raymond organized backyard sleepovers where we all compared erections. At Scout camps, boys would wait for the leaders to fall asleep before groping each other, pointing flashlights and laughing, daring someone to use his mouth, and talking trash. They gossiped about a "circle jerk" in the church men's room and about a neighbor's clubhouse where contests measured who could shoot the most, the farthest, and the fastest. Someone claimed he'd collected all his jism in a jar. I didn't ask why. It was just harmless talk, far from love or serious sin with a woman.

My first infatuation, from a distance, was Randy. When the screen door slammed across the street, I would spy on him doing chores. He was sixteen, active at church, and an athlete at school. What I felt for him had no name in the 1950s, other than admiration. Eventually he was no longer out front, washing the car with the garden hose. I imagined I too would grow up handsome, marry a woman, and move away.

* * *

I never thought about a heart attack, even as the throbbing waxed and waned through dinner. My stomach always got worse after a meal, and so I retreated to the living room, hoping it would calm down. My sons turned on television as a distraction. *America's Funniest Home Videos* came on, a program I hate, but had no energy to oppose. (Later I would make jokes about that show almost killing me.) The boys said laughter would do me good. Instead, it set off deeper spasms. Richard, now nervous, kept watching me. I asked him to rub my shoulders. He was tender, eager to please. Confused and cold, I began trembling. I had crossed some frontier; I recognized a climax and wondered whether to give in, relax, let go, but I couldn't. I couldn't bear my sons remembering me this way, quaking uncontrollably. I asked them to go to their rooms. I couldn't bear the thought of Richard left behind, suspended in time. I began to cry. Despite the chilling in my extremities and the burning in my abdomen, I cried for my three teenage boys doing homework upstairs and for Richard, who could do little more than wait.

It was a decision, not an inevitable step, to call an ambulance. I told myself to find a path through this discomfort, to somehow get beyond it. Richard made the call and then held me. I continued to shiver. At its height, each pain forced out a moan. The sound emerged from far away, and I could hear my own strange voice, apologizing. In the long minutes until the medics arrived, my only wish was to faint, to wake up on the other side.

* * *

My world as a youth knew no such word as homosexual. The concept eluded me, despite the troubling clues of difference: braininess, over-sensitivity, clumsiness at sport. In gym class, the taunting went beyond calling names to shoving, pants-ing, or a tossing into the showers, fully dressed. Then a tall boy, Jeff, chose me for his team and taught me to pass him the basketball. By high school I could guard my man, even shoot in a pinch, and the pestering subsided. I would still recall the swoop of dirty blond hair along Jeff's bare neck and think of my strong feelings for him as gratitude. Perhaps my differences would vanish once I built up more physical skills.

After other classes, the teasing went so far that one boy followed me into the corridor and spat on me as I went downstairs. Then, in high school, a straw-haired guy named Kirk chose me as his debate partner and showed me how he used his smarts to deflect attack. Before our senior year, we spent the summer moving irrigation pipe on an Idaho farm. In our migrant-worker trailer, Kirk shared the double bed with another guy. Hearing them at night, I would lie alone and feel left out. Later we went to debate camp at Brigham Young University, where I would awake in the heat to find Kirk asleep in his shorts, erect. I called my yearning for him respect. Maybe my difference would fade once I acquired more social grace.

The annoyance over sensitivity evaporated after I got to know Bill, the leader of the pep band who ate lunch with the popular crowd. He could wear a bright blue shirt with gold half-dollar polka-dots and swoon over Barbra Streisand records. I went along, even when he insisted we try out for cheerleader: "Green-white," we chanted, swinging our arms symmetrically. "Fight-fight." After we lost, he talked at a friend's house until dawn, recounting his life story, but never mentioning sex or love. Later he went to France as a Mormon missionary. I, too, entered a religious phase and went to serve in Bolivia. I would recall Bill's thick red hair as I knelt in prayer beside my assigned companion. Stripped to our one-piece underwear, our body heat commingled in the Andean cold. I had a name for my feelings then: brotherly love. My difference, I told myself, would succumb to self-mastery. I confessed to jacking off and promised myself I'd quit.

Any other course would meet with hazard. Two elders got sent home, people said, for "mutual masturbation," an intriguing possibility I had not entertained. The same occurred after I returned home and joined the Utah National Guard. Two privates in basic training got discharged from Ft. Ord after touching each other in the shower room—the most frequented spot in any barracks (the toilets sat unshielded along one wall). I imagined only the parade ground could be more exposed. In one standing joke, a soldier in formation would shout, "If you can't tap-dance, you're queer!" We all would break ranks and tap furiously—easy for anyone who once tagged along to a sister's lessons. Beyond its opprobrium, for me the term *queer* bore no special inflection (and *gay* still described a mood). Nor could I read the double entendre when the tapping itself marked the few who *could* as queer.

*   *   *

My friend Bill moved back to Europe, styled himself William, and sent me a letter from Amsterdam. He wrote to say he was gay. I felt betrayed. "Take me with you," I thought, not knowing exactly where. I went, as a college intern, to Washington, DC. Every week, I noticed a newspaper ad for the Gaiety Theatre. The suggestive poses of unclothed models excited my curiosity. I clipped out the ad, borrowed a roommate's car, and drove to the address in a poor part of town. The man in the booth said, "This is for members only," and asked for ID. In the darkened hall, finding nothing on the aisle, I tripped over someone to reach a center seat. The film was running late. In a climactic scene, one actor inserted his fist into the other's ass, to a soundtrack of guttural moans. When the sequence began again, showing the same ring of blood from a different angle, I started to leave. A man, now exposed, nearing orgasm, blocked the way I had come. Frantic, I turned and climbed past three others. At the back of the hall I stopped to catch my breath, but someone goosed me from behind. I fled.

On the drive home, my foot shook on the gas pedal and my other knee threatened to give way on the clutch. I gripped the wheel to steady my hands and took stock. Sissy and pansy, drag queen, faggot, queer—the names chanted a chorus in my head. If gay meant doing what I had just seen, then the word applied to someone else, not me. My attachments to boys in high school, to missionary companions, and to college classmates, never led to sex. My adolescent sex with other boys never led to love. The conclusion seemed inescapable: I was not gay.

My dearest friends were always women, and three years later I married one, a writer named Cindy. We met in graduate school and found we could talk forever. Once, on a ski lift, I broached the subject of gays. "If that's where they find love," she said, "you can't condemn them." We had known each other for only a month, but I longed to consummate our emotional tie. I asked her to marry me. We had a secular wedding, then drove East for our honeymoon. She got pregnant on the first night. When two more boys arrived in quick succession, friends asked if we knew where babies came from. Yes, we replied, from a diaphragm and foam, from a condom and gel, and finally from the pill. Nothing could hold us back. In the Carter recession, we couldn't find jobs and had to move a dozen times. Sex was our entertainment, until we went back to school.

When I landed my first academic job, we moved to New Hampshire with three boys in diapers. My sexual activity seemed to recede, except for the incidents. On meeting a masseur in the gym, I remarked I had never had a massage. He offered a free trial, I said fine and followed him to his office. He ended up getting me off with scented oil.

Annoyed at my own enjoyment, I protested: "Was this the usual?" "Oh, yes," he said, "the full body massage."

After another workout, as I washed my hair in the shower, someone began to suck on my dick. I froze, then gently pulled away. By the time I rinsed the soap from my eyes, he was gone. These incidents troubled me. Had I brought them on myself? Cindy said not to worry. Then, at a restaurant in New York, where William had recently moved, a man stared and smiled at me. "It's a compliment," William suggested. He took me to his neighborhood bar, where gay men cruised, touched, and kissed, and although the smoke burned my eyes, I felt completely safe.

Other changes soon followed. My new friend Rich took me to lunch and treated me, at age thirty-three, to my first glass of beer. I didn't like the taste, but I liked the company. I had no real friends in the Mormon Church. My marriage suffered as well: We stopped talking, I worked too much, our sex life went into eclipse. These symptoms left me confused and made her angry. The divorce caught us both by surprise.

* * *

At the hospital, I was shocked and relieved to find out I was having a heart attack. Finally my declining health had an explanation. I joked with the intern, with nurse after nurse, and with the physician on call, as each one asked the same questions: name, age, complaint, and pain on a scale from one to ten. I couldn't imagine worse and answered, "Ten." All their ministrations seemed droll to me. I imagined them doing group therapy to work on communication skills. When the cardiologist arrived, only to ask the same questions, I laughed. "Do you guys ever talk to each other?" I asked.

He had the gay orderly roll me into a room equipped for angioplasty. As the doctor opened my leg and worked the probe up to my heart, I concentrated on the video monitor. The image it showed made no sense to me. Through my head ran lines from a song, one that says, "seems such a waste of time," and rhymes Hackensack with "never went back"—useful nonsense when the doctor asked me to hold perfectly still. He would then expand the balloon in an artery, sending the pain off the scale, and I would hear Billy Joel singing "heart attack-ack-ack-ack-ack-ack."

Afterward, I did not feel better. The doctor explained that not only had my arteries blocked in three places, but my heart had suffered at least one earlier attack. In time new main routes had expanded along the existing capillaries. This news sent me hunting through my past. Suddenly my discomfort of recent years seemed simple, like a coat buttoned wrong. An incident when shoveling snow three years before—rushed and angry with no teenage help at hand—came back clearly. I ended up doubled over on my bed, telling the boys not to worry. The clues seemed so obvious now. I had, however, been active, cycling to work and taking canoe trips (including—now I thought of it—one spell when I had to stop paddling and wait on the shore for the spasms to pass). Rethinking my history was not as straightforward as I expected, but gave me some mental knitting to do in my hospital room.

*   *   *

With my divorce final, I moved to Illinois. Another new professor began going out with me to meet women, usually without success. I needed to take steps. First I signed up for weight training and then alternated those classes with swimming laps. In the gym almost every day, I began to notice something going on in the sauna. Without glasses, I could see only blurry shapes. Eventually one of them followed me out to the shower.

"Wait," he said. "Put your swim trunks back on."

I obeyed, embarrassed. What had I done wrong?

"Come here." He gestured.

I hesitated.

"To the unused rooms back here."

I stood still, confused.

"Oh," he said quickly, "strictly safe."

I shook my head tentatively and went back to my shower. Later he caught up with me leaving the gym. His name was Vic, and he offered me a ride. I was surprised, but curious, and he seemed harmless. In the car he made a clearer offer. We ended up talking in the parked car. I told him I couldn't imagine the romance in anonymous sex in an abandoned bathroom. Didn't a comfortable bedroom with the curtains drawn seem more appealing? He disagreed and, good as his word, took me straight home. Still, discovering that men met that way took my breath away. Resolving to pay closer attention, I wore my glasses one day. They fogged up.

Finally, I struck up a conversation with the most articulate of the sauna crowd, a journalist, as it turned out, and activist. We began having long dinners, where he patiently answered personal questions and never made a pass. From the string of close attachments to and encounters with other men, I stitched together a new history.

On my birthday, at age thirty-three, I decided. I announced to my journalist friend, "I'm going to do it." Within a few weeks, I began dating a Latino man from Chicago, and then, when he moved away, a downstate banker. I told my ex-wife.

"That explains a lot," she said, relieved. It all seemed obvious. My friend William's lover said he knew for years. My younger sister said she suspected all along. *Not so fast!* I reacted. Hadn't I loved women, fathered children? When my eldest sister called long distance, angry at my coming out, I remained impassive.

"I know what you people do," she said. "I'm a nurse!" She was right: How could mortal sin make me so comfortable and settled? My concurrence angered her more. I slid the receiver away from my ear and shrugged at my date, hands laced over his cooling dinner. What made his hinted smile, the lifted brow, the curl of one corner of his mouth, all seem so attractive? My sister never called back.

* * *

The intensive care unit, where life teeters on edge, is of all places the most banal. An incision bursting is just another way to wet the bed. Sleeplessness and bad dreams respond to simple remedies: a back rub, fresh sheets. Lights on means daytime, lights off, night, as arbitrary as a parent enforcing nap time. Food always smells better than it looks yet remains inedible despite coaxing. All this I observed distractedly.

The nurses and phlebotomists spoke to me from what seemed like a far remove, coming into sight briefly to "check the site" of the surgery or bleed my arm into brightly colored vacuum tubes. The cardiologist, at a distance, would survey my body, talk in low tones to someone, and disappear from view. I felt as if my head sat deep in a long, white cone, like the one a vet put on the neighbor's dog after surgery, to stop it from scratching the wounds.

My sons would come with Richard, fidgety from the monotony. On the phone with my parents, my lips formed familiar phrases. My mind played its inane soundtrack, replacing the frantic rhythms of "-ack-ack-ack" with something more serene, an ironic, easy-listening song with the band They Might Be Giants repeating, "I'm having a heart attack, I'm having a heart attack . . . ."

Then the nurse taught me a new trick: turning on my side to pee into a graduated bottle. No more bedpans! My sister always said life turns on a dime. I committed the error of peeing from my left side and could feel my body's weight collapsing my lung. Just then a student walked in, having ignored the "No Visitors" signs and breezed past the nurses' station. As she talked on about minutiae (my replacement in class) and youthful abstractions (the fragility of life), I found I could no longer breathe. A fit of coughing came on. Hearing the rattle in my breath, she stared, as if noting me for the first time, then excused herself and left. I coughed pointlessly, flat on my back. Exhausted by the convulsions, I pled with the nurse. She was adamant: sitting up would only reopen the incision. When the cardiologist arrived, he looked pained, pondering with one finger tapping his lips. Then, as the nurse murmured objections, he raised his hand part way, permitting me to operate the electric bed, until he signaled stop. (Perhaps this was why the nurses, mistaking my closed eyes for sleep, called him Wild Bill among themselves?) Sitting halfway, I could cough "productively" (the nurse's term). She gave me another measuring cup, and I spent that night by turns filling it up with phlegm and readjusting the rubbery respirator mask.

On the third day, Wild Bill came in, sat primly in my bed, and explained. Against poor odds the angioplasty might hold the arteries open, but a scar-tissue heart will never pump as well.

He said I came close to dying.

I said I regretted not fainting, felt cheated of my escape.

He demurred: Staying conscious kept me alive.

At that we paused.

Then he admitted he feared losing a patient so young.

Oh, I wasn't going to die, I assured him. My sons weren't quite ready to be on their own. I still had to finish my dissertation. Besides, I was taking Richard to Spain next year, in fulfillment of a lifelong dream. I thought desire alone could unblock my path.

* * *

In my first gay summer, I came out to my sons. My banker boy-friend came to dinner, greeted with a kiss: to me an ordinary peck, to him a betrayal. He was still in the closet. Uncomfortable in the presence of young boys, he left before dessert.

Over ice cream Matthew asked, "Why did you kiss that man?"

"Because we're dating—well, we were."

"But you're not going to marry him," said Joel.

"No, although someday maybe I'll find someone like him."

"But that would be gay," insisted Andrew.

"Right. I *am* gay."

The boys took sides. The eldest and youngest, Joel and Matthew, said okay. Andrew objected.

Joel said, "Drew, if Dad says he's gay, he's gay. It's not up to you."

"No, he's not."

"He is."

Despite my interruptions, this went on into the night. Andrew wouldn't budge. He explained why the next day: "Dad, you told me all your reasons, but you never listened to mine." So I listened. He said that *gay* is *bad.* It means *AIDS. Gay* is *sick.* He said, "You're not bad, you're good. And you're not sick. So you *can't* be gay." He was nine years old and triumphant. I told him I'd think about it.

On the third day, the four of us talked again, about putting people into categories, judging them without knowing them. The boys liked this adult secret, especially the "code word," *prejudiced,* and Andrew relented.

"Okay, Daddy," he said. That was it.

At the end of the summer, the boys' day camp held parents' day. The director, after the picnic, took me aside. "I just wanted to thank you," she said. "Your sons single-handedly cleaned up this camp." When I couldn't imagine how, she explained: kids can be mean, they tease and taunt, usually calling each other *gay* or *AIDS*. "Whenever your sons heard that, they said, 'You're just prejudiced,' and pretty soon all the kids were saying *prejudiced* instead."

* * *

I was naïve about homophobia, having too long reaped the straight man's comforts. When I took a summer camp (as they call cottages) in New Hampshire, the local paper ran full of letters condemning gays for AIDS. Alone in the woods, I couldn't sleep. I imagined women must feel this way walking an empty street at night.

When I interviewed for a job in Syracuse, the local press was covering a fraternity prank: Kill-A-Fag T-shirts. The dean tried to reassure me. "I couldn't have lived in New York for seventeen years without recognizing the contributions gays make to the arts." I mistook this for support and accepted the job, a step that proved near fatal.

The school had other gay and lesbian employees, none of them out at work, but that fact seemed unimportant. I couldn't believe how strange the place felt. When I went to his office the dean would remark on my dress or state of grooming. His compliments unnerved me. One of his lieutenants could not see me without petting my balding head. What did I do, I asked myself, to encourage this?

Soon the incidents escalated. After I voiced dissent in a faculty meeting, a department chair planted herself in the door to my office at eight the next day, trapping me there for a quarter hour while she berated me for flamboyant behavior. When I stood my ground, she became enraged. The following summer, hearing a plan to assign me a different office, a senior professor started a whispering campaign to keep the querulous upstart in his place. Unaware, I returned to campus, only to face the dean's scolding for this latest load of "political baggage."

I blamed myself and resolved to attend better to social matters. Yet my offers to take co-workers to lunch went often ignored and never reciprocated. After agreeing to come for dinner, a professor might simply not show up, without calling to explain. I could perceive no collusion here, no planning or conscious intent. People just seemed to find me an annoyance. The constant slights and subtle put-downs left me hurt, and the blow-ups left me feeling frightened.

At home I noticed my stomach churning, my heart always pounding, keeping me up all night. At work I kept too busy. I sat on the campus boards that brought in domestic partner benefits and that guided the campaign to value diversity. These successes helped me ignore the harshness of my own school. Falling into ill health, I never considered stress, and the doctors remained in the dark. Then came the heart attack.

Upon returning to work, triple bypass surgery and months of physical therapy behind me, I first noticed feeling nervous in the office. The doctor put me on antidepressants and sent me for counseling "to readjust." Then another incident: After I declined to host a guest speaker, a department chair began sending hostile messages by electronic mail, sometimes several a day. He accused me of carrying on a double life, neglecting my work, and harming my students. He threatened to expose me, saying he could fill a newspaper with all the facts he had on me. I denied these allegations, politely in spite of my agitation. Still the messages kept arriving. When I finally complained, the dean set up a meeting "to talk about my future in the school." Over lunch at the faculty club, he recounted the history of what he called my "social problem," upbraiding me for three long hours, until I had to go to class.

Teaching was always a relief. In the classroom, administrators left me alone. That day the topic was stereotyping, and the students, working in groups, produced a list of traits for Latinos, blacks, and the rest. When they read their list for gay men, my mind reeled. Gay men are weaklings. Hmm, so that's why people yelled at me. Gay men are vain; people made comments on my personal grooming. Overdressed: they remarked on my clothes. Sexually unthreatening: women touching my head. Interior decorators: my new office. Gay men lead double lives, molest children, and are vulnerable to threats of exposure—the students had listed my social problem. I felt stupid. How had I missed it?

I went looking for help. The sexual harassment officer could do nothing. She advised me to keep a file. The social worker from the employee assistance program did no better. She suggested I find other work. A gay psychologist proposed stress management training. Finally I went to the cardiologist. While I told him my story, he eyed me keenly and then took notes. "This case has always bothered me," he said. Oh, he'd had many patients complain of stress, but this time the diagnosis was clear. Wild Bill, true to his nickname, offered to help me fight the university.

I got lucky instead. I found a new job, in a gay supportive department in Chicago. With my sons off to work or college and Richard remaining back East, I turned to the gay community. Lots of them live in Andersonville, my north shore neighborhood, where my doctor, optician, picture framer, even my piano tuner are all gay. I go to a nearby gay bar, volunteer for a gay service project, run with a gay athletic group. I go to gay films and theater, read gay novels, patronize gay restaurants and bookstores.

Have I gone too far? I don't think so. I still carry around other selves: my Mormonism, my days in the army. Gay friends find these episodes shocking, but I've stopped revising away my own past. My period of heterosexual life I could never deny: I felt true love, enjoyed the sex, and got caught up in my sons' lives. Despite our messy divorce, I still find my ex-wife an intelligent, generous friend, the same things that attracted me two decades ago.

Being gay—that invention our tribe now gives historical substance—is my political choice. I write my congressmen, keep up with gay news on the Web, and with my friends take a stand, organize protests, and spend my dollar to support the community. When traveling I show up at gay events, just to show solidarity. I know I'm naïve. When vandals broke into my New Hampshire house—shattering windows, scattering our clothes, smashing in the TV set and microwave, slashing tires, stealing our small worthless treasures—and on their way out carved "Die Fag" in the sofa seat, I felt afraid. Instead of going to the next town meeting, I stayed home, intimidated.

Homosexual identity is all compromise. Every gay man I know considers himself an exception to the norm; likewise the lesbians. Contrary to every expectation, pushing fifty is the happiest time of my life. Start with being alive. I love exercising every day. Even my low-fat diet is a challenging game I enjoy. It makes me proud. Younger men may flirt with me on the train to work, I may still get carded in bars, but I make no secret of my age. When people guess I'm thirty-five, it makes me chuckle. Getting older feels so rich—I earned every year. The magnificent scars down my chest and leg, on my groin and palm, and across my soul bear witness. Sometimes when I walk beneath the Chicago skyline, sit in my favorite coffee shop, or rollerblade along the lakefront, I feel the mystery well up, that calm, majestic joy.

Chapter 7

Calvin

Craig Watters

I think I have always wanted to be a forty-year-old gay man—like my friend Calvin. This may not have been clear to me as I spent my free time reading about my role models, Mary Poppins and Auntie Mame. At first, they were who I thought I wanted to be and I would take these books out of the local library on an endless rotation. I used these books as character scripts. But there were only five Mary Poppins books and two or three Auntie Mames. I was severely limited in my character-development materials. I loved Mary Poppins. Not that Disney fluff of a Mary Poppins but, rather, that acerbic, starched, straight-backed English character in the P.L. Travers books. She was all business and propriety. I once dumped a bottle of my mother's lavender perfume in my bathwater just to approximate the way Mary Poppins was supposed to have smelled. I was very serious about my role-play. Auntie Mame offered all the magic of Mary Poppins, but was rich and fun and smart. I practiced this role with the help of Rosalind Russell's movie, and became quite grand and magnanimous—not attractive traits in young boys. Consequently, my mother forbade my bringing another Auntie Mame or Mary Poppins book into the house.

I may have decided to be like Calvin at the age of fifteen when Calvin looked at me closely in my mother's living room in Long Branch, New Jersey, and said to me, "You're gay, aren't you?" not as a question but as a statement. I longed to hear someone who knew what gay was say that to me. The boys in my neighborhood who called me sissy and faggot didn't count because, to them, those words meant I walked like a girl, wouldn't play football or baseball, and hung around with their sisters. It didn't mean that my crush on them could be love, that my fantasies about them went beyond a hand job in the woods. When Calvin said it to me, he knew what it meant in all of its complexity. What a day that was!

But I could have made my decision to be a forty-year-old gay man when I was about seven. I was at my grandparent's house, on the other side of town from the almost all-white housing project I lived in with my mother and brother. My grandparents lived on Liberty Street, the main concourse of the black neighborhood. Almost all of the people who walked through their door were black. I can only remember a lone white insurance man coming every two weeks to collect a payment from my grandmother.

So, it was one night when my Aunt Bootsie used my grandparent's living room as the place to host her Knit-and-Sip knitting/drinking/gossip party. My Aunt Bootsie was so sharp back then. Beautiful clothes, new car, hair done whenever she needed it, smoked Benson and Hedges that came in the box, and knew the nightlife. When I was older, I would take her out to the clubs with me where she would sit at the bar and smoke and laugh with the queens next to her.

On this night, though, I was seven and it was 1961 or 1962. Scotch and Canadian Club were on the coffee table with my grandfather's portable bar setup and ice bucket. The living room lights were low and a Nancy Wilson record was playing on the hi-fi. Aunt Bootsie was in a black cocktail dress, sipping her Dewar's with ice and water, singing with Nancy, smoking a cigarette and waiting for her guests. She was expecting many of the customers from the beauty parlor that served as her hangout, owned and run by her best friend, Miss Bessie. They all were around that thirty-ish age when voices drop from too many cigarettes and too much scotch and confidence. That's what I loved about my aunt: she had so much confidence. A friend of mine saw a picture of my aunt from around this time and said to me, "Oh, I love your aunt. Look at her face. She knows her pussy is good. Isn't that what she looks like she's saying? 'I got some good pussy'?"

And her beauty parlor friends had that same kind of confidence. As each came to the door on this night, there was no girlish cooing and giggling. They came into the house with some barely heard words said close to my aunt's ear, each voice a baritone of naughtiness and a kind of wisdom. I sat as near to the entry as my grandmother would allow me to hear and took it all in. You see, before I wanted to be a forty-year-old gay man or Auntie Mame, I wanted to be a thirtyish-year-old black woman. Not thirtyish like my mother who, at the time, was too vulnerable and tragic. No, I wanted to be like my aunt's friends. I mean, God, Miss Bessie had blonde hair!

The living room filled up with about ten women. I sat and peeked around a door to watch them light cigarettes and fix drinks. They were always laughing at each other's stories about their men or work or what happened at the Off Broadway the nights before. Their voices would lower sometimes to husky whispers and then they would all laugh loudly. My grandmother would look at me then to make sure that I hadn't heard the joke and I would pretend that I had not, just so she wouldn't make me give up my spot. When the doorbell rang this particular time, my aunt said, "I bet that's Calvin!" and went to open the door. In came a man. A big man. A big black man. A big black Haitian man with a big bag with knitting needles and yarn spilling out. I later learned that in the bottom of the bag was a rusty straight razor and a brick. A girl couldn't be too careful. He wore a long maxi-coat and a long scarf. He had marcel waves. He came through the door, eyes and mouth opened wide, and shoved his bag at my aunt. "Here' girl, take this! I gotta pee!" And he ran up the stairs to the second floor bathroom, taking two stairs at a time. Everyone screamed with laughter. I was stunned.

He came downstairs, swishing slightly as he moved into the living room. He was tall and muscular, but moved with this feline sway of his hips. His hands were huge, but it did not stop him from having an immense ring on one of his fingers or from waving them around in accusatory points and feigned slaps. His face was huge, with big eyes and lips that were almost always pursed or stretched wide as he said some biting thing that caused everyone in the living room to scream and slap at him. He moved into the kitchen from the living room. My grandfather was at the kitchen table reading the paper and my grandmother was fussing about, preparing hors d'ouevres for the living room. My grandfather said 'How ya doin', Calvin?" in a friendly voice. "Fine, Lester," Calvin boomed back at him. My grandmother was already smiling at Calvin when he screamed in a playful voice, "How ya doin', Fan?" "Stop all that noise in here!" my grandmother fussed back at him, swatting at the air in front of him. Calvin giggled and tried to catch her hand. She liked him. He swung through the little family room my brother and I were in, waving at us, then moved back into the living room where the screaming and fussing and gossip commenced in earnest. I was in love. I had seen my hero, my role model, and his name was Calvin.

By the time I was fifteen, I was seeing Calvin much more regularly. He was a nurse with my mother, and he drove her to the hospital at Fort Monmouth where they both worked. I always wished for my mother and Calvin to be assigned to the same shifts. That meant that he would come about an hour before they had to leave to hang out and eat leftovers and talk. His pronouncement of my gayness was a shock and a relief. He said he would keep my secret. But the deal included my complete abstinence from entering an active gay life until he gave the OK; that would not happen until I was eighteen and graduated from high school. In return, we could talk about his gay life frankly. I was being mentored.

Because of Calvin, I was destined never to be one of the sissies that emerged around me from playgrounds and church choirs. They were young and silly and blowing boys behind the community center. Only Wayne, an Afro'd queen from Liberty Street and his mythical boyfriend, Tony, from the next town, had reached some level of gay seriousness and were actually mentioned by Calvin from time to time.

Calvin was grooming me for gay greatness. He had experienced a lot and was ready to pass on his experience. I was never to make the same mistakes he did. That meant that I must be ready to be slapped down the stairs at the Metropolitan Opera House by my boyfriend for making eyes at the man next to me. This happened to Calvin who described the episode to me in great detail, how the blood red lining of his maxi patent-leather white coat twirled in contrast to its exterior. How the women there looked on in seeming acknowledgment that this was how it was supposed to be. I was always amazed, however, that such a big, black man could ever be regarded as feminine elegance in such a tumble. But that's what I still had to learn, wasn't it?

So, what Calvin was teaching me was realness. Not realness as a drag-queen ball category. He was teaching me attitude realness, street realness, don't-fuck-with-me-unless-I-let-you-fuck-with-me realness.

It was hard to learn. He held up his friends as examples and their lives became part of Calvin's stories. These friends had the respect of all gaydom. No one was more real, bitchier, or rougher. Isaac and Curtis were always Calvin's best friends. Isaac was the oldest and wisest of all. He worked in a laundry and always spent his money wisely. He had a fabulous apartment, a great jazz singer collection, and collected rare stamps and coins. Once, as we all sat on Isaac's Mediterranean couches and sipped drinks, Isaac sang along to a Nat King Cole song whose words were "they try to tell me I'm too young . . ." Calvin and Curtis screamed derisively. Isaac said to wait a minute and stood on his tiptoes in a closet to retrieve a gun he had hidden among some albums. "Now I'm going to sing this song again and you bitches will listen with some respect." Calvin and Curtis feigned much appreciation as Isaac sang and waved the .45 in their faces.

Curtis was the opposite of Isaac's responsible character. Just a few years older than myself, Curtis was cute and flighty, always outclassed by the older guys here but well loved. Consequently, his failures in life and love were never a big issue. Curtis was the best trainee they had. He was notoriously vicious and for that he also had their respect. Another friend, Thurston, was a drag queen and came to my mother's house in slacks and blouses and makeup. My mother once offered him a beer and he recoiled slightly at the can in her hand, saying, "Don't you have a glass?" My mother smiled and fetched one immediately.

It all seemed so far away, so impossible—this gayness of Calvin's. I could never attain it. I was never a bitch or a fighter; I smiled too easily. I never knew what a blow job was and spent hours wondering how a steady stream of my breath could be sexually desired. Calvin would laugh at me and pretend to slap my stupidity away. "Chile', listen to me" he would playfully plead, as he tried to explain things to me without being too vulgar. Sometimes I got it. I was to learn to be a bitch and a victim, a whore and church mother. The goal was to be able to move, as he did, through my grandparents' house, leave them screaming with bawdy laughter in one room while shaking hands and teasing my grandmother in another. Our deal of my abstinence was totally in line with this because it was just as he had lived his life, a learned and necessary patience. It was so old-fashioned, in a way.

Curtis became my first boyfriend. I removed my armpit hair with Nair and put on a Nik-Nik shirt for our date soon after my eighteenth birthday and graduation from Long Branch High School. Calvin watched me like a hawk in the bars and I glowed under his eye. I would step out in one-sleeved tops with bracelets, elephant bell-bottom pants, and suede wedgies, and Calvin would coo in approval. But college and the times would change all of this for me. Away at school, none of this mattered as much and I soon left Calvin's domain. I still occasionally called and he would chide me for not coming home to him enough.

Calvin died not long ago in San Francisco of some diabetic complications. He had retired by then and I was in my forties. I had spoken to him just before he left for his California vacation. One of his few remaining friends, Ralph, lived there and Calvin was thrilled to be going. So many of our friends had died but Ralph was still here. I remember, as a child, riding in a car with my mother and grandparents. We turned down a quiet street only to confront Calvin and Ralph walking on the sidewalk. Ralph wore roman sandals that laced halfway up his calves. They both were swaying and laughing when we rode by and blew the horn. I imagined that same Ralph calling back to Long Branch to tell Isaac and whoever else was still there that Calvin had fallen into a deadly coma, his leg had been amputated, and he was not expected to live. He died soon after these calls. I was so sad. But I had a dream. In it, I was sitting in a restaurant, waiting for Calvin. And when I turned toward the entrance, I saw him in the restaurant's revolving door. He was smiling, laughing at me, as he pushed the door to get inside. I laughed back and he waved his big hand at me. I think his maxi coat was still in the revolving door when he walked in. He had to pee.

Chapter 8

In the Center Ring

George Pierson

I'm now at a stage of life in which everything is starting to make much more sense. As each day passes, another small piece of the cosmic puzzle seems to fall into place.

In the mid-1970s, I was living in New York City when a good friend gave me some printed materials—a blend of Eastern and Western spiritual philosophies—that placed considerable emphasis on the idea that nothing is as it appears and everything we see is really just an illusion. According to the readings, we've made it all up—both the good and the not so good. In the years that have followed, I have come to accept the veracity of this idea through observing my everyday life experiences. Of course it was always easier to accept the good stuff. AIDS, war, innocent kids dying of cancer—more difficult to understand. In addition, at the time, I couldn't understand why I was gay.

In years past, I viewed my being gay as a deep, dark secret, clouded and layered with shame and confusion. A spiritual teacher of mine who had founded a school that taught the ancient techniques of Agni Yogi was fond of saying, ". . . everybody, regardless of what he or she is doing in life, is seeking the same thing—enlightenment." I now understand how being gay has facilitated my path toward enlightenment. As a result of relating to the various issues associated with coming to terms with my gay identity, I feel I have moved closer to an enlightened state of consciousness. I now see my being gay as a gift—a gift from God or the universe.

I am now in my midfifties, and feel happier and more fulfilled than ever before. I experience a greater sense of wonder and joy and have integrated my life values into a single source of energy that helps me respond more creatively, wisely, and with compassion to every aspect of my life, both professionally and personally.

Being able to accept myself more completely has allowed me to be more accepting of others, regardless of who they are. As I am able to more fully honor my journey—rather than curse it—I am able to do the same for others' journeys as well. I can more quickly and more easily drop any self-criticism and judgments of others. I find myself to be a better manager of others as a result and feel a greater sensitivity and compassion for their struggles. I've come to realize that life isn't easy for anyone and we're all in this thing called "life" together.

Feeling more inspired has created the dilemma of having too many interests and too little time to do all that I want to do. For me, this has become one of the primary remaining "problems" of my life as I feel as enthusiastic about the future now as I did when I was a teenager, if not more so.

As a teenager, I—like most—was strongly influenced by peer pressure; the need to conform was enormous. Growing older has made it much easier to let go and just be who I am. I have come to the realization that most people have their own plates filled with their own stuff and don't have much time to spend thinking about what's on yours.

Looking over a half century of experience, I can see several benefits to my having been gay. First, I feel a greater sensitivity to all that happens and this has made my life richer and allowed me to age more gracefully. Second, being gay has facilitated my passion for creative thinking, and finally, it has enhanced my spiritual awakening. Once you turn fifty, these factors become increasingly important to you. This seems especially true in a culture in which so much emphasis in placed on youth, appearance, and physical gratification. I assume I will never lose interest in things of the flesh, but I am able to see them in their proper perspective—at least most of the time.

My creative development started years before I was really conscious of sex. As a very young child, I knew I was different and had interests that differed from those of my four brothers. I was always curious as to why I felt this way and this drove me to find answers for no other reason than to reach out for a greater sense of inner peace.

I was the firstborn to a newly married couple, and there was a great deal of friction and upheaval in the family throughout my childhood. I hated it. I would always withdraw into my own private world to avoid taking sides when things got really intense. I just wanted to disappear or, at least, be perceived as neutral by everyone involved.

My sensitivity to the feelings of others led me to do whatever I could to not be the cause of suffering for someone else. Most of the time, I just wanted to escape to a secret castle in my head, and I used my imagination to create a world in which I wanted to live. This inner world helped me to survive my childhood—even though my family was very dysfunctional, my childhood, for the most part, was happy and filled with excitement, adventure, and imagination.

My escapes at will into fantasyland opened the doors of my creative mind that might have remained closed otherwise. It has served me well through a successful career in television promotion and design. By unlocking an inner world of creative imagination, these escapes stirred my passion for creative expression in many areas.

At one point, my inner reality and an external event came together. When I was five years old, we lived in the small town of Opa-Locka (just north of Miami). One morning, a small army of trucks appeared. They stopped right across the street from our house. Men exited the trucks and began setting up a big-top tent. A real circus was being set up across the street. Every inch of the sandy lot was filled with weird people, props, costumes, elephants, and other exotic animals—all framed against a bright orange-yellow carpet of freshly shoveled sawdust. I was thrilled. Heart-pounding circus music filled the entire big top over the roaring sounds of generators.

What I saw was a group of grownups who were making their living just trying to make other people happy as they traveled from one town to another. I decided then that joining the circus and making others happy was what I wanted to do when I grew up. Somebody else would have to grow up and be the fireman. I had other plans.

Long after the circus rolled out of town, I would wander around the vacant lot where once-prancing horses had left their imprints in three rings in the sand. I would replay the joyous experience of the circus over and over in my head. Even today, I can recall this experience as if it had happened yesterday.

Although I did not grow up and join the circus, my passion for it remains as strong as it was then. I go to every show that comes to town, and my home is cluttered with circus toys and memorabilia.

From my perspective now, I see that what was so appealing about the circus was the diversity it promoted. The stranger the better. In that environment, even I could be accepted. It was a good ego boost to me as a child; it mirrored my own imagined world. Several years ago at a seminar, I had a flashback in which I realized that the childhood circus experience had been the first inkling of an awareness of my "secret"—my homosexual desire.

Perhaps, the secret was a bit more obvious in my childhood act, "George and Tommy." Tommy was my ventriloquist's dummy (and perhaps, my first gay relationship). I wrote my own material and performed at my elementary school. In the script, Tommy would make me "accidentally" break a raw egg on my head. After every performance, I would take my only suit to the dry cleaner to have it cleaned. I was too shy to tell the owner what the egg stain was about. He must have wondered as I brought the suit in over the course of several years—the shy kid and the egg-stained suit.

I also expressed my creativity at the movies, in particular, big epics such as *Ben Hur* and *The Greatest Show on Earth* (there's the circus again). I was eight years old, and would take a nutcracker to the Saturday matinee movie. I would pretend to edit any boring parts in the movie (mostly the love scenes) with a simple squeeze of my nutcracker.

As a teenager, I would occasionally seek out information about homosexuality at the library. What I found initially were statements indicating that it was something I would eventually grow out of as I matured. One medical journal in the late 1950s stated that the reason young boys engage in homosexual acts was simply to satisfy their curiosity about the male genitals. The authors suggested that more exposure to other boys' genitals would cause these unnatural desires to vanish quickly. Some advice for a kid like me.

Other materials said that homosexuality was a mental illness. It wasn't until my early twenties—in the early 1960s—that I found anything that spoke positively of homosexuality. It was a small paperback book that I found in a shopping mall in North Miami Beach. As I read the book, I felt an immediate warm glow of self-acceptance flood my entire body. It was such a relief to know that I wasn't the only one in the world with these feelings. I felt free—at least on the inside. For the first time in my life, I felt like I might be a normal human being. At the time, I had no idea how long it would be before I could externalize those initial inner feelings of love and self-acceptance into my everyday life.

This initial opening to accepting myself—cracking the door open—helped me start my spiritual quest. For me, spirituality is about seeking the truth. I could not come out of the closet without first telling myself the truth. I had to challenge some fundamental beliefs about life and to go against a number of societal norms. The sexual revolution had not even begun in the south during the 1950s and early 1960s.

When I first came out, it seemed that the gay social scene centered around the bars. The bar scene never worked for me—I grew bored with it and ventured off into new learning experiences. Even though most of these activities involved a focus on self-improvement and spiritual growth, and despite my initial experience of self-acceptance, I went back into the closet for the better part of the next eighteen years.

At the time, three death-related experiences pushed me forward on my spiritual quest. The first was John F. Kennedy's assassination. I was in art school at the time. The following summer, my father died after a long illness, and a month later, I was involved in a near-fatal traffic accident in the middle of the Everglades on my way back to school. These experiences led me to ask several questions including, "Why is life worth struggling for if you're going to end up dying anyway?" I also puzzled over the fact that I had come within a split second of death and, yet, had survived without a scratch. Did my life have an unknown purpose to it? Did I survive for some reason?

My sunny disposition went into a tailspin that lasted for years. When I graduated, I took a job at Hallmark Cards in Kansas City and set out in my new beige VW Beetle from Florida. Shortly thereafter, Martin Luther King Jr. was assassinated, then Bobby Kennedy (who was a hero of mine). Then there was the Vietnam War, and the riots in Chicago at the Democratic National Convention.

I wanted to leave the country, but I was in the Air Force Reserve. I did the next best thing and moved to New York City. I arrived on Halloween 1968 (just before the election of Richard Nixon—another grave disappointment). I stayed with a friend who was an illustrator whose apartment was on the Lower East side. I felt as if I had come home—at last. Here was a city filled with strange sights and a diversity of people—it was just like the circus.

In 1969, the Stonewall riots occurred. I was at ABC-TV working as a graphic designer, and began to feel restless. A few months later, I responded to an ad in the *Village Voice* to participate in a weekly gay encounter group. The group was led by a gay therapist and was held at his Upper West Side apartment every Sunday afternoon. I would sometimes show up still in uniform after spending the weekend with the Air Force Reserve.

Six months later, I found an ad in *The New York Times* that changed the direction of my life. The ad offered an introduction to Silva Mind Control. Being both new to the city and somewhat naïve, I assumed that if it ran in *The New York Times,* it must have some credibility. I scraped up $150 to take the course—$150 was a lot of money for me at the time. I wanted to get my money's worth so I practiced the meditation techniques religiously. During lunch, I would go to Saint Thomas Church and practice. I'm glad I did, because this changed my life. My experience in the course led me to quit the gay encounter group—which I was growing bored with—and to venture off into an investigation of the world of consciousness.

During this period, I read just about every metaphysical book and took any related seminar that came to New York City. Name just about any metaphysical approach and I've probably done it. I did everything but drugs. I found I could get high enough without them. Besides, I wanted full value for all these seminars and the techniques they taught. All this led to greater clarity and insight about my life and pushed me to keep exploring other growth opportunities.

After years of doing countless workshops, seminars, and all types of classes and spending many months in India, I still for the most part remained in the closet. It wasn't until my forties that I realized that unless I came out of the closet, my spiritual quest would be suspended. I signed up to take a gay men's spiritual workshop called "Honoring Our Journey." The workshop provided me with an opportunity to look back on my life and celebrate the journey I had taken thus far before starting on the path anew. It was during that workshop that I realized that being gay was the catalyst for my spiritual quest. Everything was brought home to me. All my gay and creative identities could be integrated into one—linked together with my heart and soul. All my identities started to live together for the first time. There is the often-held belief that an external relationship will make one whole. My experience made it clear that "connecting within" would make me whole.

Today, the neighborhood in Washington, DC, where I live has a large gay population. In the midst of this gay-positive area, yet without a lot of fanfare and effort, my friends and I are helping one another define and redefine what it means to be gay.

As I look back on my life, I now see how each step I chose on my journey and how everything that has happened had a purpose and laid the foundation for the next step. Even the detours appear to have served a purpose. My desire now is to reach out to others—regardless of sexual orientation—who could use a helping hand. By being less constrained by what is rigidly defined as normal or even as real, I feel freer to experience the miracles that life has to offer.

Chapter 9

Voyage to Ithaka

Michael Ross

Setting out on the voyage to Ithaka you must pray that the way be long, full of adventures and experiences.

Cavafy, *Ithaka*[1]

Is the glass half full or half empty? Is one at midlife or middle-age? Is a person gay or homosexual? Three weeks after I reached forty, often considered the beginning of midlife for gay men, my lover of nearly fourteen years left me. It happened on a Saturday morning on one of those clear, warm Sydney early summer days, two days after I had sold the house that I largely owned with him. His mother (and more recently his father) had died, and he had said, "Why don't we sell this place and buy a better one with the money from my parents' estate?" So I did sell it, at the loss of over half my life savings, which I had put into it. The morning after the sale was finalized, my lover told me that he had never had any intention of buying a new house. He told friends that he was angry because I was wanting to start into my academic career again (I had left a tenured position to move to Sydney with him as he started his own academic career). They told me that he was insanely jealous of having a lover with a more successful career than he had.

Unfortunately, I was still as much in love with him then as I had been when we first met, a week after my arrival in Adelaide straight from my post-doc in Finland. When we met, I was embarking on my first academic job: he was a junior (at another university in the same city) although slightly older than me.

After his brutal pronouncement, I spent that day and night at a friend's house, numbed, distraught, and sobbing. I returned home the next day after picking up a hefty prescription of sleeping pills, some plastic garbage bags, and rubber bands. My ex-lover was visiting his sister that day. I had taken my first mouthful of pills when I remembered that I had left everything to him in my will.

Divine providence covers a lot of situations. I called my sister in Melbourne, intending to tell her that I was changing my will and where to find it. As she asked what was wrong, I broke down. With that intuition only someone close could have, she said, "Don't do *anything*. Leave the front door open. I'll be there in two hours." She raced to the airport, caught the first plane leaving, and was holding me before noon. I guess that divine intervention comes when least expected, but I owe my life to my sister. She took me back to Melbourne, and within a few days I was acutely ill with hepatitis A—too sick for weeks to do anything but walk to the bathroom twice a day. Perhaps that too saved me.

> *You must always have Ithaka in your mind, arrival there is your predestination.*
>
> Cavafy, *Ithaka*

When I went into a gay bar for the first time in fourteen years, I was no longer a fairly attractive twenty-six-year-old but a bald forty-year-old—and about as welcome as if I had walked into a fundamentalist church with a banner demanding gay marriage. As a gay object of desire, I was if not dead, at least left feeling as if I should seek out some necrophiliac club. I had to radically reevaluate what being "gay" was all about. Is being homosexual a state or a process? A point of definition or the vessel for taking a voyage of discovery? Browning, in *A Queer Geography*, quotes an Italian confidant as saying that "My homosexuality is neither the starting point nor the point of arrival for me—and it's not the address of arrival."[2] Where homosexuality is defined as a state of identity, and where that state is conceptualized in terms of sex and attraction to and for other men, then becoming less attractive is an approaching identity death.

I think that this may encapsulate the dilemma of aging and being gay—that we become so defined by our own master status that we also create our own psychological holocaust. By "master status" I mean the identity which can define most of what we do—where the things that we do are defined by ourselves or by others as being this way *because* we are gay. As Frank Browning comments, "As a tactic 'outness' is quick, direct and effective, but as an ideology or even a strategic program, 'outness' is empty. It offers no particular linkage between our relation as human beings (politics) and the mysteries of our psychic selves (our aesthetic coherence)."[3] Little wonder that I felt actively suicidal for months.

There was a point at which I decided that life was worth living again. I was having lunch with a dear friend on Oxford Street in Sydney, recovering from hepatitis, and for the first time in many months, I had some alcohol. As I sat drinking a champagne cocktail in the inebriating blue of an Australian autumn day, and faced with the care and concern of friends, many of them my graduate students and work colleagues, I decided that life could still be lived. That is not to say that the emotional freeze engendered by the reaction of the gay community (personified by the inhabitants of gay bars) was completely melted by the response of my friends. A year after Peter had left me, I had a beautiful relationship with a man who I had known as a workmate for several years—and my inability to accept that I was lovable led me to terminate the relationship when I left to work in the United States. In retrospect, and coming at the point where I have regained a sense of self-worth, that was one of the decisions in my life I regret most.

So my mental health has come to be based on being un-gay—not in the sense that I have retreated into the closet or denied that I am gay, or even regretted it. I now see being gay as the vessel in which I am taking a voyage, not the point of arrival. I am not defined solely by my attraction to other men. Instead of value being determined by the laws of supply and demand in the sexual marketplace, I have an intrinsic value which is unfolding. As the Dutch Catechism argues, "The authentic enlightenment is to be sought not in the beginning but in the course of things and their culmination."[4]

> *But do not hurry the journey at all. Better that it should last for many years; be quite old when you anchor at the island, rich with all you have gained on the way . . .*

> Cavafy, *Ithaka*

If I do not define myself in terms of being loved and valued by others in the context of a gay relationship, where does my value come from? I am sitting in the Empire Café and at the next table, three women are poring over bridal magazines. The overelaborate sameness of the wedding dresses takes me back to the televised image of a fairytale princess emerging from a carriage at Westminster Abbey like an explosion in a toilet paper factory. Myth and aftermyth. It is the relationships in my life that have given the defining points, but now I don't see them as being measured by the mythical (both in heterosexual and homosexual myth), all-or-nothing standard. Love is nice, but it has to come from within me first to elicit any reflection outside me. And sometimes the telephoto-like focus on one individual can blind us to the beauty of the setting.

> *Ithaka has given you your lovely journey. Without Ithaka you would never have set out.*

> Cavafy, *Ithaka*

I am very grateful for being gay. It has given me the opportunity to have a fulfilling career and intellectual life, without a wife, children, or heterosexual conventions, with the necessity and the ability to question and not to take any of it for granted. Such questioning also raises problematic issues about being "gay"—that is, having the master status of being a gay person, which defines the way many people see me and sometimes how I see myself. But I see being gay as incidental to much of my life, and as also being responsible for some of the midlife issues that I grapple with. We criticize internalized homophobia—heterosexual antigay values fungating within—as the enemy. Perhaps in coming out, as young adults, this is true; in middle age, I have seen the enemy, and it's us. The people who reject us when we are no longer young and beautiful (if we ever were) are other gay men, not heterosexuals. Edmund White, in *The Farewell Symphony* refers to standing around in gay bars and cruising as "the ultimate sad-sack act of self-hating narcissism."[5] In an Eriksonian upheaval of psychological magnitude, we are shown the way out of the Garden of Eden in much the same way as old Eskimos, a burden to their families, are sent out on the ice to freeze to death. And if we have not been able to develop social supports or other meanings in life as an alternative to being valued for looks or sexual marketability, then our vessel founders.

> *Be quite old when you anchor at the island, rich with all you have gained on the way.*

Cavafy, *Ithaka*

Un homme d'un certain age. The French understand that elegance, wisdom, sophistication, and that certain *je ne sais quois* do not end in one's forties. They are more likely to start there. They are something your soul raises up before you on the voyage. I feel much more comfortable with a clean-shaven head than with those wisps of desperation trained over a bald spot like the aftermath of basket-weaving therapy in a ward for psychotics. Cavafy's *Ithaka* is a voyage of adventures that enrich the soul, where one does not settle. Tennyson's *Ulysses* is so enraptured by the voyage that he leaves Ithaca again despite his old age: "The long day wanes: the slow moon climbs: the deep moans round with many voices. Come, my friends, 'tis not to late to seek a newer world."[6] For me, the meaning of life is in the living of it, not in trying to force my life into the glass slipper of myth and narrow prescription. We are not, of course, told how Cinderella managed to walk in glass slippers when they did fit. It must have been like trying to ballet dance in fishing waders.

> *Many be the summer mornings when with what pleasure, with what delight you enter harbors never seen before.*

Cavafy, *Ithaka*

At this age, I see my life as a series of journeys, not a single one. Actually, as a series of flights. Just as my aircraft points its sharp muzzle toward the runway, the deepening whine of the jet spooling down behind me signaling the transition from wolf to dog, I know that on the next flight, at the end of the same runway, it will be quivering back on its haunches, about to be transformed into a wolf again. That magical time between wolf and dog is a psychological period, not a temporal one.

I had learned to fly in the Air Force, but becoming a penniless graduate student stopped my flying as surely as a sidewinder missile would have. Six months after I thought my life had ended, I was in the pilot's seat of an aerobatic trainer with the frosted azure of the Warragamba Dam beneath the tail fading into the smoky haze of the Blue Mountains. As the far horizon lazily rotated around the aircraft's nose in a slow roll, as I was pressed into my seat by the force of four gravities and freed as the horizon rose above my head as the loop tightened, the importance of life 4,000 feet below disappeared. The flashes of gold wattle and silver stream in the valleys far below looked like precious metals pulsing in the veins of a mine.

Six thousand feet above Galveston Bay, the air sighs over the Perspex cockpit like the claws of a dragon caressing a crystal ball. The propeller flickers rhythmically like swift fingers strumming a great lute. Reeling out of a cartwheel and straight down toward the tangled, muddy slug-like trails of the shrimp boats far below, I understand the meaning of an Ithaka. I pray that the way be long.

NOTES

1. Cavafy, C.P. (1971). *Poems by C.P. Cavafy.* J. Mavrogordato, transl. London: Chatto & Windus.

2. Browning, F. (1996). *A Queer Geography: Journeys Toward a Sexual Self* (Revised Edition) (p. 79). New York: The Noonday Press.

3. Browning, F. (1996). *A Queer Geography: Journeys Toward a Sexual Self* (Revised Edition) (p. 103). New York: The Noonday Press.

4. *De Nieuwe Katechismus.* (1966) K. Smyth, transl., 1967 (p. 263). New York: Herder & Herder.

5. White, E. (1997). *The Farewell Symphony* (p. 328). New York: Alfred A. Knopf.

6. Tennyson, A. (1991). *Selected Poems* (p. 96). London: Penguin.

Chapter 10

Dutiful Son, Dutiful Friend

Frank Wong

This is the second time I have written a personal memoir—the first time was about ten years ago for a book to help families and friends better understand sexual orientation. This time, I agonized a bit more about what to say—a great deal has happened over the past decade. I didn't really think about entering midlife until reminded by my friends and my mother.

The oft-repeated phrases—"beauty is only skin deep" and "don't judge a book by its cover"—have long described how I feel others perceive me. I don't wish to give the impression that I am some kind of Adonis (I am not), but I have been told that I look "forever twenty-nine." I jokingly say that it must be the rice. People who do not know me well (especially when meeting me for the first time) tend to perceive me as a young and naïve person. I suppose for many (particularly among members of the popular gay culture in North America) this would be considered flattering. However, from a Chinese background in which old age is tied to wisdom, the perception is not entirely complimentary.

I have begun to realize that physical appearance and age, as well as secondary qualities such as status and responsibility, have affected the way I conduct my professional and personal life. I must confess to spending a lot of energy making sure that people know about my academic credentials and professional achievements—to leave no doubt that they are talking to an articulate and intelligent person rather than some "exotic Chinese boy toy."

More recently, my mother (who became a widow in 1981) reminds me on a regular basis that I am "no spring chicken." For a Chinese woman in her late seventies, she is extremely liberal and understanding—she simply wants me to settle down with a "nice chap." She was quite disappointed when I broke up with my ex-lover. She says that I work too hard and don't enjoy enough play. What she does not say is that although she understands about the changing times and cultural environment, I am not exactly a dutiful son in the eyes of the extended family. My mother does not need my financial support, but she did grow up in an era in which there was a strong belief that a family should not be apart. As the matriarch of our immediate family, she has the right to expect my brother (the firstborn boy) and me to be at her side, preferably living with her. By marrying, my sister is no longer considered part of the "original" family although she remains very close to the family. It is my brother's and my responsibility to take care of our mother. Old age comes with status in Chinese culture as well as responsibility depending on one's role in the family. My brother and his family live with my mother in Canada. I, on the other hand, have opted to pursue my dreams associated with my career in the United States.

I am not sure that my mother fully comprehends my desire for a career. I can't fully explain to her my need to have a life that is independent of her. During a family gathering this past year, I said to my brother and mother that I was aware that the life I have chosen for myself would not have been possible were I the firstborn son. I deeply appreciate what Tony (my brother) has done to take care of our mother and my mother's tolerance for my choices. However, a part of me feels that I have failed.

Being a dutiful Chinese son also means that one follows his father's footstep and sticks to family traditions and heritage. Both my paternal and maternal families come from generations of the influential mercantile class in Hong Kong and the former South Vietnam (especially on my father's side of the family). I have chosen a career in the social and behavioral sciences—a career that oddly enough would have been approved by my paternal grandfather who was a social activist. My career choice means I will never make the amount of money that my father did. Unlike most of my cousins, I do not have an elaborate lifestyle. I have been criticized by my extended family for this although my immediate family has supported my choice. Much of the criticism has focused on my not being a dutiful Chinese son and that it reflects on some failing by my mother. My mother is a very spiritual woman and, for the most part, is not concerned with what other people think of her. Even so, I feel guilt for somehow having failed her as a son. I know it would please her more to see me settle down with a significant other rather than follow some archaic Chinese traditions. Yet heritage and tradition die hard and I am not immune to them.

This sense of trying to be the dutiful Chinese son is more important to me as I grow older, and my identity as a gay person in midlife has assumed a less prominent position—at times even a conflicting one. I am out to family and friends, and at work. I am not sure that my mother and siblings fully understand my desire but they more or less accept me as I am.

However, being a dutiful Chinese son involves having children, carrying on the family name. I know of many Chinese gay men who lead double lives—"married with children" leading a closeted gay life. I told my family that this was not an option for me. I also don't feel a particularly strong desire to have children. I suppose it is a disappointment to my mother that I will not pass on the family name and perhaps she worries that I will not have someone to take care of me when I am older. I have never asked her directly if this is how she feels. Telling her that I wanted a life of my own was difficult enough. Maybe some things are better left unsaid.

Until recently, I felt that I was either going to be alone or perpetually dating for the rest of my life. While I do have a fairly large circle of gay friends, my workaholic tendencies leave me little time (and often little patience) for cultivating and maintaining an intimate relationship. I was to move in with my ex-lover, but out of the blue he called to say that the relationship was not working for him—he felt that I put my career before him. He was right; there were probably plenty of signs that it was not working that I had been unwilling to see.

As a result of the breakup, I worked even harder and longer hours. My career became my primary identity. I moved from New York to Boston where I worked for five years. Last year, I returned to New York City. On balance, the move has been very good for my career. In my current position, I do not feel that I have to constantly prove my worthiness. I also feel more comfortable socializing and trying to have a life beyond my career.

This venture into a life beyond career has been challenging. In some ways, I feel as though I have been ignoring my Chinese heritage. I was born in South Vietnam, moved at the age of six to Hong Kong, and at age sixteen, moved to Canada where I finished high school and went to college. My primary exposure to Chinese culture and history was during those ten years in Hong Kong. I was the intellectual kid in the family and can still master the classical readings—I am probably the best at this in the entire extended family. My desire for a career that is not part of the family history can be troublesome. I am a hard worker and I know all the long hours are, in part, an attempt to prove to the world (especially my family) that I can make it on my own and that I am a worthy person. A large part of my identity is wrapped up in my academic and professional accomplishments. The long hours are also an escape from having to think about the many obligations and responsibilities of the dutiful Chinese son. Perhaps, if I am exceptionally good at my work, my family will be able to overlook my failing as a dutiful son.

Despite hoping to find a life beyond work, I found that from 1998 to 1999, my life resembled a speed dial telephone in constant action. Shortly after the move to New York, my boss and I took a business trip. I had met my boss, Mark, a few years earlier at a professional conference, but did not get to know him well until I took the position as the founding Director of Research and Evaluation at the agency where he worked.

Mark was a very passionate, proud, and stubborn person. We became good friends very quickly. We lived in the same neighborhood and spent a great deal of time together. At the time, he had been in his position for about ten months and was experiencing a lot of stress. I was a sympathetic listener—mindful that Mark was my boss. His stress was compounded by his poor health due to AIDS. His mood could be volatile. At times, I even wondered how much control he had of his faculties.

Toward the end of February 1999, Mark decided he could no longer work and decided to quit. He had no other immediate employment prospects. Meanwhile, I became aware that he had been in conflict with his landlord. Shortly thereafter, he was evicted. It was a difficult time for him—professionally, personally, and spiritually. Fortunately, he was well regarded professionally in the New York area, and he was able to very quickly find consulting work. He moved in temporarily with me on March 24 and put his belongings in storage.

At times, it was difficult for me to separate the professional from the personal with Mark. After his departure from our agency, he maintained a consulting agreement with the Executive Director. I insisted that I would not be the one to oversee his work in light of his being my houseguest.

Mark was the most brilliant grant writer I have ever known. Almost every grant he wrote in the past fifteen years was funded. I am also a fairly decent grant writer and our collaboration was only natural. In the meantime, I asked to serve in Mark's old position. This, however, created a good deal of friction between Mark and me. Initially, he felt that I had betrayed him. I tried to reason with him that he was not being fair and to try to be objective given the circumstances. He had decided (with no input from me) to quit after all. I still needed to do my work regardless of his decision. Eventually, Mark relaxed about the situation.

We spent Mark's forty-second birthday writing a grant in front of a fireplace at the house of his childhood friend, Tom, in their hometown in Upstate New York. As usual, we had numerous disagreements about what to put in the grant. I was still getting to know Mark and was intrigued by how he interacted with Tom—he seemed like a different person. It was the first time I came to see the Mark that I would come to know as passionate.

Mark was a wonderful roommate—and a gourmet cook. With my additional responsibilities at work, I often came home late. Dinner was always ready when I got home. Without any effort, Mark and I established a routine. We spent a lot of time in the kitchen talking about whatever came to mind. We talked about his estranged relationship with his mother who refused to ever acknowledge his intelligence (he had gone to Colgate University on a full scholarship), and with his brother (always unemployed) with whom he had not had a conversation since age sixteen. We also talked about the provincial mentality of the people in his hometown, about Tom's generosity and unflinching friendship, about Mark's spiritual dilemma, including a brief stint in a religious cult, and about his living with AIDS. We also talked about his loneliness and his lifelong desire to help those who have no voice in our society.

At that point in time, life seemed to be working for Mark even though his health had its ups and downs. I was also more or less aware that I had become his caretaker and that anything could happen at any moment. One of those moments occurred when he was in extreme physical pain because of an allergic reaction to medication that resulted in swelling of his legs. He had wanted to die in that moment. It was difficult to see him suffering. I talked with him throughout that night.

By April, he had saved enough money for an apartment of his own. Despite having the money to move, he continued to live with me. We were enjoying each other's friendship and company.

On May 17, we finished another grant. He had been coughing for over two weeks and I knew he would be upset if I acted like a "mother hen." I tried not to say anything about the cough but that evening he said in a very calm voice, "Frank, I think I'm getting sick again." I called his doctor and accompanied him to the hospital. He insisted that I bring my laptop computer with me so that we could finish the grant we were working on. He was in great pain but also seemed to be in a relatively good mood.

He finally got to his hospital room at 4:00 in the morning—we had been there since 9:00 the night before. I spent the next six days in a haze. I had two business trips scheduled, but soon realized that I could not complete those trips. Mark appeared to be recovering, but I felt I couldn't leave.

Mark had another good friend, Shelly, who had been his former boss. Both Tom and Shelly lived in Upstate New York but they were in constant contact with me during this period. Mark also spoke to his mother once on the phone. Then suddenly, his condition got much worse. He called me at 7:00 one morning and wanted me to come to the hospital immediately. He thought he had experienced a psychotic episode—the first he had ever had. He was very scared. His doctor was there when I arrived and, after some discussion, Mark assigned me to be his medical proxy.

It was a difficult day for both of us. At times, Mark was lucid but then there were times when he thought he was seeing phantom people. I often was at a loss of words with him. During a brief moment of clarity, Mark wanted me to reevaluate my decision to care for him. He said, "I hope you understand the burden and the consequences." It was not easy for Mark to ask for help or assistance from anyone. All his life he had been most proud of his independence: leaving his hometown and graduating from college with distinction. He had spent his adult life providing and caring for the less fortunate. I came to understand his statement not only as a concern for my well-being but also as an indication of his trust in me. He often would say, "You always mean what you say." Somehow those words led me to recognize that I was in love with him.

It was a long day—twelve hours in the hospital. I needed to get some rest. Before I left I told Mark, "I love you." Mark said, "I love you, too." Then, he started seeing things again in the room.

Once home, I called Tom and Shelly. I then thought I should take a shower. It was after 10:00 p.m. and as I began walking to the bathroom, I felt Mark's presence in the apartment. It was a very strong sensation and it startled me. Shortly after 11:00 p.m., Mark's doctor called to say that Mark's condition had deteriorated. I called Mark's mother for the first time, explaining to her what little I knew, and told her that I would do my best. Another doctor called at 1:30 a.m. to say that Mark was now in a coma and was in the intensive care unit; the hospital staff had been trying to stabilize Mark's condition for the past four hours.

Shelly came down from Albany the next morning. The day turned into one test after another. Meanwhile, both of us were preparing for the worst. We spent time talking to the insurance company and attending to other details. Mark's condition continued to deteriorate. Before going to dinner with Shelly, I gave authorization to the doctors to pump the fluids out of his heart. I received a page while we were at the restaurant and was told that Mark was dying. Shelly and I consulted with the doctors who told us that additional medical intervention would not help Mark. I knew that Mark did not want to be put on life support, so I agreed to let him die. It was the most difficult decision of my life.

Shelly and I went into the intensive care unit to see Mark. Other than all the tubes, he looked calm, but a bit pale. The doctor said that Mark could hear us but could not respond. Earlier that morning, I had given Mark a Buddhist amulet. I taped it to his arm. Other than our sobbing, the only other noise in the room came from the machines and Mark's breathing. Someone, Shelly or the nurse, mentioned to me that there were tears in Mark's eyes. Indeed there were tears—the first I had ever seen him shed. I wondered what Mark was trying to tell me at that moment. He died within the hour.

I began making the funeral arrangements, including informing Mark's estranged family. His mother came down with Tom for an intimate private funeral—a total of about fifteen or so friends. It was an awkward meeting with his mother. I was upset that upon being told of his death, she responded that the earliest she could come down was the following Thursday. Shelly and I arranged the funeral for that Friday. I offered to let Mark's mother go through his possessions, but she said she did not want any of them. I was stunned. She also complained about his cremation. Mark had told Tom a long time ago that he wished to be cremated and to have his ashes spread around a ravine. I told myself that she had no right to object to the funeral arrangements, as Tom, Shelly, and I were his family as well.

As a Hinayana Buddhist, the arrangements were all new to me. I was told that I should have a memorial card for Mark. Knowing Mark's feeling about religion, I picked the only card that had no overt reference to God but that did talk about charity and quoted Corinthians 13:4-7. I found the card on Tuesday. Searching through his belongings the night before the funeral (Thursday night) for material to use in a eulogy, Shelly and I examined his computer files. We found an unfinished essay dated April 28 (year unknown) in which he wrote about himself. It read *born and raised in the Roman Catholic Church, I retain what is best in that tradition—charity.*

Mark, thank you for your love.

Chapter 11

The Choice

Trevor Southey

I am gay and late middle-aged. I find myself surprised that I still often feel torn between two worlds. I don't quite fit into either as they are. Each is alien in its own way. But then, perhaps I am alien within my species—alien in the way of the eccentric, the odd man, the peculiar person—and would remain so even if I did belong more completely to one of these worlds or the other.

I am also aware that as a gay man, I am in a happier place for gay people than has perhaps ever been. However, lest we become complacent, I think it interesting that while I am in the middle of exploring my place as a gay man at middle age, I should still find myself shocked by the bigotry that some of my friends from years ago hold. Their bigotry is not without personal consequence, as it causes me to bring up the old debate that I once entertained about whether or not I would take a pill—if available—to change my emotional and sexual desire.

The bigotry came to my attention when a friend from my closeted days accidentally sent me a group e-mail letter about a beer advertisement that was gay sympathetic. In pious outrage at the "wantonness" of such a thing, the friend was appealing to others to contact the company and lodge a complaint. In her letter to a friend named Michael, she wrote:

> Incidentally Michael, for the record, I am not homophobic. I have some very good friends and relatives who are gay. And some of them are among the nicest people I know. I simply

object very strenuously to the PROMOTION and therefore the increasing acceptance of the gay lifestyle as being "normal." Trevor Southey and I have had many extremely frank discussions about this. I've also told him: I love him very much, but I abhor his lifestyle choice! And yes, I've had strong debates with him on the subject of whether or not it *IS* a choice. And we have had to agree to disagree on the topic."

In a letter to me, she wrote:

And Trevor, what I WISH I'd also said to Michael, is that while I still love you and think you are a wonderfully warm, caring individual, I still firmly believe that homosexuality is WRONG. Following in Jesus' example to me means that we are not to sit idly by and allow what we consider "sin" to become acceptable.

Just as an aside Trevor, I also feel that it is within our rights to register our "vote" of disapproval of the ad—just as gay people had the right to register their approval of it—otherwise it's discriminating against OUR viewpoint! Anyway Trevor, I am really sorry again that this came to you.

Love, Natalie

She also wrote that the basis of her beliefs was based on the statements of various religious leaders, including Jerry Falwell.

The question that immediately came to mind, was "Why do I even bother with a person who ABHORS my lifestyle?" Unfortunately, her attitude still brings to the surface some of my own insecurities and unresolved issues surrounding my own sexuality and it only adds fuel to a nagging fear that the current generally improved state of affairs is one that may not last. I only need remember the "tolerant" world of pre-Nazi Germany to understand how easily all the gains made over the last several decades could be swept away with breathtaking speed and violence. I hope that society at large will come to understand and embrace the idea that it is just about love, but I cannot guarantee that such a shift will occur.

How does one respond to the level of ignorance expressed by Natalie? I have chosen to engage the battle by focusing on the concepts of "choice" and "lifestyle," as for me and those I know, it has not been a conscious choice. I wrote to Natalie that her involvement and support of a man like Jerry Falwell was disturbing. To me, Falwell is a man who is directly responsible for the types of attitudes that lead to torture and murder of innocent people such as Matthew Shepard. Although Natalie had the right to express herself actively on this issue, she needed to realize the consequences of her actions. I also pointed out the importance of acknowledging her individual responsibility for her thoughts and actions as follows:

> You really need to think as to what this is all about. Ask yourself some questions and then answer them yourself with your own native intelligence. Ultimately you are responsible for your conclusions. Saying that others told me this was the way does not absolve you from the responsibility of very careful and independent thinking.

Her argument has always been that homosexuality is a choice and later in the letter I wrote:

> I am absolutely certain, BASED ON MY OWN LIFE and that of all the homosexual people I know, that we awakened to [the] reality [of our sexuality]. We did not adopt or choose it. I know that this is fundamentally in direct conflict with and repulsive to your belief system and that of many other religions and non-religious systems. Hence, you would quote your church leaders. I would remind you and all those others who are certain of such bigotry, that within the last several hundred years alone, horrific inhumane treatment has been inflicted on millions of people because of such absolute certainty derived from sources such as the Bible.
>
> Now I want to tell you a little about my own life in regard to this matter of choice. Remember, I was born and raised in a true backwater, then Rhodesia in Africa. I had only instinctively and gradually realized that I was in dangerous waters when my affectional proclivity and then my sexuality, slowly revealed itself to me. I must have heard the word "queer" sometime in my late teens and sensed that was my place, a place of discomfort

and shame. In time I would understand that practicing the love I yearned for had criminal import. I could not allow this to be. I emphasize, Natalie, when I was a young boy in Rhodesia, I never even heard words like "homosexual" or "gay." Nevertheless, it was well before puberty that I sensed I was different. I had a crush on my cousin Terry when I was seven or eight, but had no idea what that was all about, only recently identifying it. Ironically, I found out much later in life that his twin, Pat, and his older brother were also homosexual, and have lived out their lives in loneliness, terror, and shame.

So just when did I make this choice? Was it as I watched from a distance this older cousin, Terry, and yearned for him to hold me? Was it later when I joined the Scouts and had a couple of masturbatory experiences with a boy who was undoubtedly straight? Remember, there was no book, no picture or "lifestyle" which could influence me or promote that way. Was it when I found myself compelled by the beauty of the male body in magazines a couple of years later? (Why was I not compelled by pictures of women in bathing suits?) Was it when I had my first real homosexual experience when I was sixteen, which I found horrifying and frightening? Instead of gently leading me, this man perhaps assumed that I was experienced, and became too aggressive too fast.

While at art school in England, I discovered more. Because I was so afraid of it, it was only a sordid glimpse into that world usually only governed by lust and fraught with danger. I have only learned in my maturity that, in Brighton at that time, there was a very potent underground society to which I might have been introduced. Instead, I discovered that public toilets were a magnet to we who were ignorant and hidden and lonely, like myself. Knowing no other alternative, I would, sick with fear and excitement, make occasional forays in the hope that I might meet someone. But for a variety of reasons, most of those who haunted such places were furtive and seemed only interested in quick erotic encounters. Again, why did I go to such places? I suppose I should be ashamed, but I am not. There was no other place that I knew of to go.

Ironically, when I did meet a person who might have introduced me into the healthier world, it turned out to be another painful encounter with a more mature man. Was it this experience that pushed me over the edge?

Or did I make that choice when I was walking down to class one day with my roommates and one of them, a cheerful fun-loving girl walking behind me suddenly called out, "Southey, you walk like a queer"?

There was one brief, promising almost romance with a young Royal Air Force man. But I went home for a summer and when I returned, I somehow failed to properly connect with him. Was it some deliberate failure born of my fear?

Was I turning my back on this world [because I was] stubbornly committed to the world of "normalcy?" I wanted a wife and children, a home in the country, and a normal life. I sought therapy and was told that all I had to do was learn to walk like a man, talk like a man, maybe even play a sport, and I would become that wonder of wonders, a real man. And then, if I married, everything would assuredly be fine. So in spite of the other possibilities, I declared no, "This year I am going to be married."

So I was. So here I was, denied the natural affection and love by the CHOICE I had made to be straight.

As Natalie had known my wife, Elaine, I then wrote a great deal about our marriage and our attempts to deal with my confusion and anxiety about my sexuality. I had told Elaine about my feelings for men before we married and she—like me—was convinced we could overcome them. I then went on to write:

I have never ceased to regret the pain I inflicted on Elaine. She is a naturally physical and affectionate person who did not deserve to be drawn into the drama of my soul searching. But I do not flagellate myself either. We were both victims of societal ignorance and bigotry more than anything else. Our marriage lasted fifteen years and was very loving in the way of sibling affection. She was a devoted mother to our young children. She even yielded with enthusiasm to most of my wild ideas in the early years. We did indeed build the kind of paradise of which I had dreamed, as much in the place as in the family that we were. She eventually felt, perhaps, that she had become a slave to my vision while she was denied the ultimate intimacy because of me.

I languished in my own inner misery as the years went by, even though the stage of our lives grew more wonderful and most of the other players seemed to thrive. Yet I was being destroyed. Finally, I had to make the CHOICE, the choice to follow nature. For me, it was devastating. The love I have yearned for has only manifested itself briefly five years ago, and proved to be full of woe because the two men who became successively my companions were so shattered by their own trauma of lies, secrecy, and finally, CHOICE. By the way, these were very young men who offered a world much more informed and hospitable than my world of a couple of decades before, but still a world of too much shame.

It has taken me fifteen years to even approximate the quality of life I enjoyed as a married man. My career was set back at least ten years. My children have on the whole come through very well, but they had to endure untold misery. Worst of all was the pain inflicted on Elaine. Fortunately, she has been able to carve out a brilliant career for herself and is married to a man who truly seems to adore her. My CHOICE seems to have been right for her.

And Natalie, I hate to break it to you, but even though you are polite and even friendly toward my kind, you are homophobic; you consider homosexuality to be abhorrent. Since sexuality is core to the character and very being of people like me, you are, whether you like it or not, homophobic. You despise my way of expressing love. I understand why. But this is not a "behavior"; it is simply that, an expression of love. I do not really expect this long and wordy document will change your mind. But I do hope you will do one thing for me. Keep it and read it every now and then.

So, here I am at nearly sixty trying to make those who proclaim they love me understand that they must involve the fundamental me. Otherwise the love is so conditional as to be completely shallow.

Fortunately, I do experience love. My children are now grown and outstandingly close to their openly gay dad. Even so, I wonder about the course of my life and what it is to be a man near sixty in the gay world and in the world at large.

It is lonely for me. Why? Perhaps because of my demanding and erratic success as an artist. Perhaps because I ended up being a single father to three of my four children as they successively decided to join me in California where I had moved three years after I divorced. Perhaps because I was horribly insecure, believing for most of my life that I was a lesser creature. Perhaps because I refused to pay the price of the standard of beauty demanded by my subculture. Perhaps it was because I did not feel comfortable in the usual places of meeting people and was anyway very bad at the courting games.

Whatever the reason, I did not know the complete romance which I had left my wife and children to find until ten years had passed. I glimpsed it in a few unrequited experiences, but did not know the stunning, consuming sense of completion until relatively recently.

It is lonely for me. Two much younger men over the last six years made it clear to me that I was desired. Surprised and then delirious, I quickly accepted the proffered love. Sadly, the chaos of my life and their own inexperience and insecurity proved fatal for those relationships that seemed to hold so much promise. One remains a friend, the other, for whom the passion was the most strong, has become distant. I have only briefly known the ultimate intimacy for which I sacrificed a "normal" life. I cannot deny a degree of bitterness toward both worlds.

Nevertheless, being gay makes me the father that I am, being gay makes me the friend that I am. Being gay makes me the artist that I am. Being gay makes me the citizen that I am. Being gay infuses all aspects of my life and being. Although I am a man of as much folly as any other, I believe that my view of the universe, the planet, other humans . . . everything is through the lens of my total being. And it is a good view. Core to that being and as much the heart of my soul is my sexuality. The view is unusual within the larger world and invaluable because it is relatively rare. It is not because of its peculiar source that I have been hurt by it; it is because most people do not comprehend its unique nature and its capacity for good. It is seen as exclusively sexual and perverted.

Certainly, some aspects of life would have been simpler had I not been gay. But lost would be that peculiar view of life, a view that has made and makes now enormous contributions to the well-being of other people. The richness of culture alone is in debt to many such as myself. Some are famous, but most are probably lost to the mists of time, hostages and slaves to secrecy and shame. But they still left behind enormous legacies of art, literature, music, science, government, etc. There is no question in my mind that the subtlety, enormity, and significance of these contributions was born to a large extent by the sexual and affectional nature of these people.

For me, so much life lies ahead as I become more whole with each passing day. Dreams of what can be unfold in me constantly. Dreams of creating places of tolerance and vision. Dreams of using my work to awaken the hearts of those cold in arrogance. Dreams of using the power of the special insights that being different gives one to infuse all that can be reached, and reaching beyond the easy, with good and power and a sense of a future full of wonder.

I envision a utopia that will be a place of gathering. It will be first a beautiful place environmentally. It will be architecturally intimate. It will embrace all kinds and all ages. It will provide stimulation in arts, philosophy, athletics, etc. But it will also be a pragmatic place, realistically facing social dilemmas such as unusual families, abuse, and aging. It will always be an organic place, always flirting with new ideas, but it will use history to make growth thoughtful and careful. I am glad to be thinking of such a place and I know that would not be happening without the unusual nature that I have. I relish that nature.

So, my lot is peculiarly mine. Probably the most peculiar thing about me is my sexuality, which, I believe, largely defined my other idiosyncrasies. This was true when I was young, and is still true today. Thanks to the courage and strength of many, it is seen as less peculiar by more and more people, if not by a majority. And although my world has become more my own to command as I have grown older, I am still a rare bird. Sometimes this is exhilarating when I dream dreams such as those above. But it is also often a lonely place to be.

Chapter 12

Tesoro

Michael Segovia

Ten years ago, my mother sobbed that "it was her fault" that her only son was gay. Her *tesoro* (translates to *treasure* from Spanish) was tainted in her eyes. My father took an even less logical approach: that "it" ran in my mother's family—two cousins, two second cousins, possibly a great aunt, a few others. They couldn't understand how their *tesoro* had fallen into this group. They set ground rules that I was not to talk about it whenever I came home to Texas from California. No one in the family was to know. This was going to be our little family secret. "It wasn't fair," my mom said when I protested, "You can go back to California, but we will have to deal with what everyone says back here." So, to get back at them, I made it a point not to go home. I stopped going home for Christmas. I stopped calling. I decided that if my parents didn't want me as I am, then I didn't want them.

I told my parents I was gay at that particular point in time because they were heading out to visit me from Texas. I made a conscious decision to not pretend to be straight anymore. I didn't want to pretend to notice or be physically interested in a woman as she walked by. The Saturday morning before their trip, I picked up the phone and dialed home. My father answered. I was relieved that he answered. He has always been very calm. I hoped that would continue over the next few minutes. I remember most of the words we used as if it were this morning. I didn't practice beforehand. I just shot from the cuff. "Dad, I need to tell you something. This is something that almost everyone in my life knows—everyone except two of the people I love most—you and Mom. I'm gay," I heard myself say. This was followed by about ten seconds of pure, painfully loud silence. "I guess I've always known," my dad finally answered. He followed with, "Mijo, I have said that I have always loved you and I always will. This doesn't change that." "What about Mom?" I asked. "I'll handle your mother," he replied. I was very relieved now. Although my father was always calm, my mother can tend to be a bit—okay, more than a bit—emotional. I can say this because I take after her in many ways, including this one. After a few more words, my father and I hung up. I sat in my room, dazed. I couldn't believe what I had done. I felt so free. Then I realized that in only a week, I would have to deal with this all for real—in person—face to face. What had I done?

Four days passed, and my oldest sister called. She and I had already had the "I'm-gay" talk years earlier. She said that our mother had been crying since Dad told her four days earlier. My heart fell to the floor upon hearing this. The thought of ever making my mother cry made me feel like the worst person in the entire world. Now I had really done it. Three days to go before they arrived. Would they still come?

The day before my parents arrived, my father called to let me know when they would be getting to my house. I asked how my mother was doing. He uncomfortably said she was doing okay but not great, and wondered if they should still come.

The next day, I was upstairs in my room moving furniture around with a work colleague when I heard the doorbell ring. I left the front door open, because we were moving furniture in from his house to mine. I looked down the flight of stairs to see my mother's sweet face peering into the doorway calling, "Mijo, it's us!" I ran down, and my mother hugged me long and hard, with only a trace of a tear in her eyes. My dad followed with a hug equally as special.

During their stay, I tried a couple of times to bring up the phone call, but each time my parents motioned for me to stop. They knew, but that didn't mean they were ready to talk about it.

Eventually, we began to talk about it. It was not that visit, however. It took several other times together to actually bring it up again. But it was very clear at that point that they did not like the idea. That was when the unwritten, but even more powerful, rules were expressed by them as to how I was to behave as a gay man in their lives.

Further, I was feeling frustrated that I could never live up to the conditional expectations I had let them place on me.

I walked into my therapist's office soon after that and told him I had a dream that my mother had died. I woke up sobbing, terrified. He looked at me with his typical smart-ass look and said, "So, you wish your mother was dead." I was shocked. "Of course not," I countered. It wasn't until a week later that I realized he was right. I hated that he was always right. I was very angry at my mother and father for not accepting me for who I was. I was also hurt that they didn't understand seven years ago how much my heart ached when I told them that Mathieu and I had broken up.

Two and a half years later, when John and I broke up, my mother at least asked, "Why?" when I cried to her over the phone. She quickly changed the subject when it got too detailed for her. Meanwhile, I took every opportunity I could to let them know that I was not dropping the subject. When my mother came out to California to help take care of me following a knee surgery, Mathieu was also there. One day during that visit, I asked her if she would like to go to church. "Of course," she gladly said. I didn't tell her until we arrived that the church was Dignity and that the members were primarily gay and lesbian. (I didn't even mention transgender—too much at one time I think.) Ironically enough, one of my favorite ministers, Sharna Suthern, gave a sermon on the acceptance of alternate lifestyles in families. My mother and I sat there in the front row and listened (I thought) to the same sermon. I was moved to tears. When it was all over, I asked my mother, "What did you think?" "I liked the music," was all she said. She pretended not to really hear or understand the rest. At dinner following church, we waited out in front of The Sausage Factory on Castro Street when right on cue a guy in leather wearing chaps and no butt covering walked right on by, showing his bare ass to all of us. My mother turned red (hard for a dark-skinned Latina to do) and hid her face. I had to laugh as I realized I had taken her into all of this on the same day as the Folsom Street Fair!

But, now a decade after I first told them I was gay, both my parents realize that this is just part of who I am. They welcome Steve, my partner of five years, into their home and they have been out to our home twice. They will be here this December in California to spend Christmas with us for the first time. They enjoy talking to Steve on the phone often, even if he is, as my mother warmly jokes, a *volillo* (white bread). They appreciate that Steve is my partner for life and even more, they respect that. They encourage it. At Christmastime, a large box arrives from my parents with two wrapped presents. One is for me; the other is for Steve. Recently, a package came in the mail addressed only to Steve. It was a ceramic sun face for Steve's garden. Steve put it up right away, and it looks beautiful overlooking the garden. But for me, the more beautiful sight was the smile on Steve's face when he first realized my parents had sent the gift specifically for him.

When my parents last visited, they both made it a point to learn about Steve's life. I was touched when I heard Steve and my father in the living room laughing together, sharing stories (some embarrassing ones about me), and just being comfortable together. Of course, Steve helped to make it easy for them. His friendly manner and natural style of relating to people are very special. His sense of humor didn't hurt, either. On a sightseeing tour of San Francisco, he might have gotten carried away with his humor. We were driving toward Market Street when another car cut me off. I slammed on my brakes. Steve yelled out "Maricon!" in the other car's direction (*maricon* is a derogatory word in Spanish for gay—it translates to something like "faggot"). Of course, he yelled it so only those in the car could hear, but those in the car were my parents. They both got very quiet for a few seconds. My mother finally asked my father, "What did he say?" My father, holding back a chuckle, told her. Nothing else was said, but by the looks on their faces, I could tell that they appreciated the comment for whatever bizarre reason.

During that same visit, Steve and I had a party at our home where we invited different people from our lives. We made it a point to include both gay and straight friends. Several colleagues from work were present. This was a well-planned attempt to show my parents that other people were comfortable with us as a couple and that, basically, other people saw Steve and I as simply two people who loved each other.

I can't give all the credit to Steve for helping my parents grow more comfortable. My previous boyfriend, John, had a lot to do with this as well. He showed me what I should not only expect, but what I should demand from my family in terms of acceptance and respect of my lifestyle. He demanded this of his own family, and while they didn't like the idea, they came to the startling realization that if they did not accept him, they were going to lose him. I came into all of this with John's family while they were in the midst of deciding how they were going to deal with it. I remember visiting John's family for the first time. They didn't seem too happy to meet me. It was John's mom who came around first. She, John, and I went to brunch one Sunday morning and talked. She listened, she talked, she made it a point to work through her issues about her son being gay and his new boyfriend sitting right in front of her. From that meal on, it was John's mother who was the first to include me in not only her family functions, but any of the relatives' (including her in-laws) family functions. I look back at those times and I miss them. And I think about what an interesting picture we all would have taken. John's family was very white. In the middle of all this "whiteness" was this Mexican guy. Over time, the rest of the family accepted us.

One Easter, we were all over at John's parents' house enjoying a large family gathering. There is a tradition in the household that each married couple would pose, one couple at a time, in front of the fireplace, while John's dad took a picture. John and I sat in the living room watching television, wondering without admitting to each other if we were going to be called. Breaking the silence of our inner thoughts came the booming voice of his father calling our names. We got up pretending to innocently wonder what he wanted. He motioned us over to the special picture-taking spot. John and I stood about a foot apart, looking a bit shell-shocked by it all, when his dad barked out through the camera lens to John, "Get closer and put your arm around him." I could have cried. I was so touched. I never did tell his dad how much that meant to me. Maybe one day, I will.

Toward the end of our relationship, my parents decided to take a trip out to California. They knew I was seeing some guy named John and they knew that we were living together. My sister called shortly before my parents arrived to tell me how nervous they were about coming to visit me and my boyfriend. They weren't comfortable with the idea that John and I might kiss or be overly affectionate in front of them. Little did they know that I wasn't comfortable with it either.

Once my parents spent a day or two around us, they relaxed. They realized that nothing was going to be thrown in their faces. I noticed them watching us. They were curious, I guess, as to how two men related in an intimate relationship, especially since one of the men was their son. John was good with my parents. He was very engaging with people anyway. He tried hard to win them over, and I will always appreciate that.

Although John had a lot to do with my parents' acceptance, Steve added yet another level to all of this. John tried very hard to gain acceptance and succeeded, but Steve let it come to him. He is, as I said earlier, just a naturally relaxed person. Now that is not as easy as it sounds. I believe that many of us have a tendency to question or deny people's acceptance or respect. We tend to dismiss it as false or as being based on misconceptions. I have those inner doubts. You know the one: "If they really knew me they wouldn't accept me." Steve doesn't seem to have that baggage. This makes it easy for people to accept him, to respect him.

So where are we? How did it come to this a full ten years later? Could it be that my parents finally realized that their little boy was no longer a little boy—now almost forty. This is the life that has chosen him and that he has chosen, and there is nothing they can or should do about it.

I am grateful now for all that I have experienced with my parents. I am glad that I have been able to realize that there are no two people that I respect and admire more. I know that all of this has not been easy for them; nor has it been for me. But I also know that they love me enough to question what they were taught by a world that just doesn't understand. I almost prefer that it hasn't been easy. We have passed a true test of what family is all about.

A couple years back, I met the great American poet Maya Angelou in a restaurant in Dallas. I walked up to her and asked her for an autograph. She held out her hand and I offered mine to shake. She shook my hand, and then held it with both of her hands the entire time she spoke to me. She asked my name, and when I told her she asked, "Like the guitarist?" (Andre Segovia) "Yes," I answered, "but I don't have half his gift." She responded, "But you have your own gifts, dear."

As I approach forty, my personal gifts are more apparent to me now, but there are also "other" gifts—the life that Steve and I have built and the ongoing relationship my parents and I are developing. They still call me their *tesoro*. I now call them mine.

Chapter 13

This Body

Jeff Siebert

Several months ago, this body of mine hit the half-century mark. In recent years, my life has taken me on a spiritual journey that has opened doors I didn't consciously know existed when I was younger. I can't say that I've passed completely through those doors, but I am trying to look at what's on the other side. At the same time I am trying to clarify issues on the side where I still seem to find myself much of the time.

The older I get and the closer my body seems to death, the more the age-old question "Who am I?" seems relevant. I now believe that any answer to my life's ultimate dilemma—that it inevitably will end in death—lies in how I answer that question. Ironically, I spent a good part of my adult life trying to hide who I thought I was—an effective way certainly of blocking any real answer. I'll return to that issue later.

Looking back, I remember at sixteen hoping I wouldn't live to be twenty-one so that the awful secret of my homosexuality would not be exposed. I was certain it would become obvious as I grew older and the pressure to lead a heterosexual life increased. For a while, I thought "spirituality" might give me an out—the priesthood could be a place to hide. But I never actively pursued that option. In my sophomore year in college, I left the Catholic Church, largely because of their condemnation of homosexuality. But I felt no need to explain myself—it seemed most college students in the 1970s were abandoning the faith they'd been raised in. I guarded my secret.

I did seek counseling later in college. The social worker felt that my homosexuality was simply a self-image or identity problem—I was a skinny kid who didn't excel in sports, so how could I feel masculine with such a body? He suggested I try weightlifting at the gym. Feeling muscles beginning to bulge for the first time in my life gave me self-confidence that I had not experienced before. It also began a stage of narcissistic preoccupation that has not yet completely subsided. I really did like the idea of being masculine and behaving in masculine ways and that opened me up to the idea of dating women. It may not have been who I was, but it was a self-created image of myself that I was beginning to value, even enjoy. My desire to be normal, to have a "normal" heterosexual life, was powerful—so powerful that I denied what I was feeling at a deeper level in order to fit in. I was a psychology major and the behaviorists supported my belief that I could make myself over—with the right reinforcers, behavior was almost infinitely malleable. My question then was not "Who am I?" but "Who or what do I want to be?"

By twenty-one and my senior year in college, I had a girlfriend and found that, thanks to youthful hormones, my body could respond sexually simply from physical contact. It was such a relief to find that my cover actually worked. In my first year of graduate school, I sought additional counseling after my first homosexual encounter. My roommate in student housing was gay and he had patiently "seduced" me over a period of several months. In therapy, I was told that masturbating to *Playboy* could redirect my sex drive. This occurred during the early 1970s, when homosexuality was still considered a psychological disorder. I believed it.

Twenty-five seemed to be my most difficult birthday. I had felt that twenty-one was my peak, and now I was rapidly going downhill, halfway to thirty. At the age of twenty-six, still hiding, I married a young woman who had been a student in an undergraduate course I had taught. We truly enjoyed each other's company, never ran out of things to talk about, and made each other laugh a lot. She was my best friend. I loved her then—still do—but I could not bring myself to share my shameful secret with her. During our eleven years together, I never acted on my attraction to men. We worked closely together in our joint careers at the university where I was hired after graduate school. I found much satisfaction in this seemingly successful image of normalcy. Despite its apparent effectiveness, I experienced on-going feelings of tension, anxiety, fear, and guilt—the strain of trying to keep hidden from others, including my wife, but not myself, the thoughts and feelings of the despised self that I thought I really was.

When my wife fell in love with someone else and asked for a divorce, I was crushed, and terrified that my secret would at last be exposed. But I was surprised at the same time to feel a sense of relief, even excitement. Until then, I had spent my life trying to live as I thought I was supposed to, projecting what I thought was an appropriate image of myself. Now perhaps, I thought, I might finally be able to find out what I really wanted and who I really was. I had no sense of the deepest ramifications of that thought.

I did have an unexpected intuition almost immediately that my coming out sexually was somehow related to my spirituality, despite my contrary feelings that my sexuality was sinful or evil. While I was dating two men, both practicing Catholics, I returned briefly to the Church, long enough to realize I would not find answers to my vague search for spiritual meaning there. But I found it helpful to revisit the religion of my youth and make peace with it so that I could begin looking else-where.

I knew enough about gay culture as I was coming out to suspect that, at age thirty-five, I was over the hill in terms of youth and beauty. I didn't expect to have much success in dating. But I was still youthful-looking and again built myself up physically, so that I was not lacking for dates. Still, several younger men who were initially attracted to me turned away when they discovered my age. I was beginning to experience the effects of aging in an age-conscious culture.

I developed a new self-image as a confident, open, gay man. When a gay friend offered to educate me about what I needed to acquire in terms of dress and interests to be part of the gay subculture, I pro-tested that I was not looking simply to conform to a new set of exter-nal standards in place of the previous ones I was now relinquishing. This was my opportunity to find out who I was and what I really liked and wanted, no longer making my own desires and wishes subservi-ent to the goal of being normal.

I anticipated that all my previous anxiety, fear, guilt, and pain would now lift and dissipate. Hiding my sexual self was the problem,

I had believed, so accepting my homosexual feelings and coming out to my family, friends, and colleagues should have been all I needed to do to find peace of mind. But I was wrong. There were more layers to peel back, more levels to disclose, at least to myself. One of them was allowing myself to come out of the closet spiritually, which seemed in many ways an even more difficult step to take in an academic environment than revealing my sexual orientation. I had been aware of vague spiritual yearnings and interests when I was in graduate school and had read some Jung, as well as some pop psychospirituality such as Carlos Castanedas and Joseph Chilton Pearce. I had put it all on the back burner while I pursued a career in a setting that was at best oblivious and at worst hostile to spiritual concerns.

But now I knew that had to be my next step, although I did not have a clear idea of what spirituality really was. A psychic friend introduced me to the idea of channeled material, such as Jane Roberts' *Seth*, which I evaluated primarily in terms of whether the book was saying anything that I intuitively recognized to be true and universal. I really didn't know what I was looking for, or even if it existed. I resonated to the idea of dimensions beyond the physical, and to statements of the pitfalls of judging either ourselves or others. I knew I would have to live my life very differently if I really embraced those ideas. And then, when some open-minded colleagues told me about a spiritual teaching called *A Course in Miracles* and I borrowed the book, I recognized that I had found what I had been unconsciously searching for. The words in the Course touched me deeply and I had a strong sense that I was reading "truth," despite my great difficulty comprehending much of what I was reading. I was uncomfortable with the assertion that the words came from Jesus, so I decided that initially I would simply evaluate the validity of the message itself and concern myself with authorship later. Yet I kept waiting for the Jesus of the Catholic Church to appear on the next page and condemn me for my recently accepted homosexuality. Instead I found a completely nonjudgmental, totally loving and accepting presence. I realized that this Jesus was going to say absolutely nothing about my sexuality, as I sensed that he was addressing me at some other level. It would take years before I would really begin to recognize the level at which he was speaking to me and that it would help me answer more deeply the question, "Who am I?"

I experienced joy and peace in the words I was reading, yet they did not bring an end to my pain, fear, or guilt—rather, they led to an exploration into the depths of those emotions. The Course literally turned my life upside down and I took a leave of absence in 1988 to work at a center that offers support groups for people dealing with various kinds of life crises, including life-challenging illnesses. The center operated on principles derived from the Course and was located just north of San Francisco.

I moved to San Francisco just before my fortieth birthday. I felt it was no coincidence that I was relocating to gay mecca, that I could have the best of both worlds, and perhaps even meet the man of my dreams. I had been attempting to ignore that my hair was getting progressively thinner and that I needed reading glasses. My aging process had actually seemed to accelerate shortly before I left Miami when a young man with whom I had become infatuated told me I was too old for him. I'd never felt so old as I did with that rejection. As I was aging, I was increasingly experiencing the downside of a gay culture obsessed with youth and beauty. Yet I still wanted to play the game, hoping to stay youthful-looking long enough to develop a satisfying relationship with an attractive young man. There was a contradiction there, but I wanted to be the exception.

I spent four years in San Francisco and met a number of wonderful gay men—developing very deep friendships with some. But I did not meet the love of my life. I began to realize that it perhaps did not matter where I lived and that, most important, I needed to follow my intuition to wherever it seemed to be leading me. That apparently was to a center in the Catskill Mountains of rural New York State called the *Foundation for A Course in Miracles*. So in late 1992, I flew to New York to join the staff. My belongings followed in a UPS truck.

I've not really been as isolated as I thought I might be from the gay community here. About a year after my move, I learned of a new gay spiritual retreat house that had opened not more than twenty minutes from where I live. This has allowed me to continue to explore what it means to be a gay man with other gay men, in an eclectic spiritual context. Perhaps because fewer young gay men have been attracted to this spiritually based center, I've been somewhat sheltered from the typical experiences of growing older in a youth-oriented culture. Yet my own attraction toward male youth and beauty persists.

A couple of years ago, a friend shared a delightfully provocative quote that was placed in the mouth of Socrates by Plato in his dialogue, "Charmides." When I read how Socrates "caught fire" at a glimpse beneath a beautiful youth's cloak, I decided to explore Plato's thoughts on male love and beauty. I discovered a book that gathered all his major writings on male-male love and friendship. I found the *Dialogues* enlightening and affirming. For example, in *The Symposium* Plato discusses the attraction toward individual physical beauty as a reflection of a deeper yearning for abstract beauty and truth. He argues that the deeper experience comes not from denying the attraction to the physical, but by accepting it so that eventually we can transcend it, remembering the absolute beauty behind all appearances, which are only pale shadows of the reality.

The most helpful realizations in answer to my search for self-understanding have come from my work with *A Course in Miracles*. Insights seem to keep coming to me at deeper and deeper levels. One of the major ones that I only alluded to earlier is that the words of the Course are addressed to me as a mind and not the body and personality that I think I am. Much like the figure I seem to be in my dreams at night, the self I think I am with this life history of challenges and struggles to come to grips with my identity, is no more real. Now that's hard to accept, let alone experience, as the truth. So maybe I'm not ready to embrace that assertion wholeheartedly. I've had to ask myself if I'm willing at least to consider "What if it were true?"

What if I'm the dreamer and not the dream figure? It follows then that I, as the dreamer, am responsible for the content of my dreams. That also can be hard to accept. It means I'm no longer a victim to forces, events, and people outside of me. So I've had to ask myself, why am I dreaming such a painful, loveless dream? A unique contribution of this spiritual path is that, steeped in psychological insights, it goes beyond other spiritual paths that also assert that the world and our lives are dreams to tell me why I'm dreaming.

The answer takes me even deeper into who I am and farther away from my specific daily experiences as this physical self. I've found glimpses of this reality to be still extremely rare. But even the dreamer is not who I truly am. Spirit is the only reality—an abstract, limitless extension of love and peace, beyond all concepts of time and space. My dream is a dream of separation and individuality, but my reality is perfect oneness. To dream of separation is to choose limits and opposites, and to reject love. That, were it possible, would have to be very painful. But to protect the dream and keep it going, so I can maintain a separate, individual identity, I have to see my pain as not in my mind but in my body, with its cause outside of me in the other figures and events of my dream rather than in my choice to dream. The aging of my body, as it loses its vitality and attractiveness, then is an inevitable outcome of my life, over which I have no control nor am in any way responsible for, if this self is who I am. Certainly, when I awake in the morning and reflect on a frightening or disturbing dream, it is apparent that my own mind has chosen to present this experience to me as if it were something happening to me rather than something I was choosing. I know from personal experience then what tricks my mind is capable of.

In practical terms, I'm not yet ready to let go of my individual identity. However, I am learning increasingly that I can at least begin to consider the possibility that my interpretations of events impinging on me, or rather, on the self I still think I am, must be wrong, since my judgments are always coming from the perspective of the dream figure and not the dreamer. That willingness to begin to question my judgments is what the Course means by forgiveness, and that is my way out of the dream. I am learning, little by little, not to take the events of my life quite so seriously. That means less guilt, fear, and pain and so my willingness is growing. I will awaken when I'm ready. Now at least I can begin to put my life experiences, as a fearful, closeted gay man, into perspective. If this self has been a cover to protect my individuality and not take responsibility for my pain, then hiding aspects of my self throughout my life has been a very effective strategy for avoiding any meaningful consideration of the question of who I am. And though I may have felt separate and different from everyone else, I could say that it was not my fault. My desire to be normal, to be like everyone else, may have reflected a deeper yearning for joining, but it was clearly coming from a sense of condemnation and guilt directed toward both myself and others. Thus, beginning to accept my sexual self as part of my identity was a necessary initial step that I needed to take to progress spiritually. It was by no means a final answer, but it was an essential part of the journey. So long as I was judging any part of myself as unacceptable, I could not move to any deeper level.

And now my issues related to being a gay man with an aging body have become my lessons in forgiveness as I seek to open up to an awareness of my identity at a deeper level. Near my fiftieth birthday, I noticed some probable arthritis in one of my fingers and scheduled a colonoscopy because of family history. I'm finding it amusing that we give each decade such very special significance—we count this way, in base ten, simply because that's how many fingers we have. I'm also amused by the excessive focus on the millennial year 2000, since we count our years in the Western world using an estimate of the year of the birth of Jesus that most biblical scholars now agree is inaccurate. Maybe we have, as the Course says, made it all up and given everything in this world all the meaning that it has, including our age as a measurement of the passage of time. On one hand, this idea could be depressing, but then again it may offer a way out. If I've given everything all the meaning that it has, perhaps there is another meaning it can be given. And perhaps all the meaning I give anything only depends on how I answer the question, "Who am I?"

Chapter 14

Sense of Place

Christopher K. Bramwell

I was born in 1958 on an Air Force base in San Antonio, Texas. My family and I didn't live there long, and I have almost no recollection of that time except for a church picnic when my mother found me floating face down, motionless, in the slow-moving Salado Creek. I was three. She had been a lifeguard and jumped in the chest-high muddy waters to pull me out, not knowing if I was dead or alive. Word of the near-drowning spread and at church the next Sunday, someone asked me how I managed to float until my mother found me. I said, "Heavenly Father was holding me up."

I was raised Mormon, an upbringing that profoundly shaped not only my sense of self but, unexpectedly, my sense of place. Dad was an Air Force pilot and we moved frequently; I loved the nomadic life with its regular new adventures. In my twenties, a friend who doubted the value of that life for a child asked, "But how could you ever develop a sense of place?" I was speechless because her question felt logical and yet I didn't feel "placeless." I wondered how that could be when I moved every two or three years. The longest I lived anywhere growing up was six years, a tortured eternity! And yet, strangely, I felt a sense of place even when I couldn't say where.

I've since come to understand my parents' careful devotion to their faith provided me the unplanned and unexpected byproduct of a sense of place that was not specifically physical, as in a town or state, but a place in a familiar community nonetheless.

With news of each military transfer, the family gathered around a map or a globe and my parents excitedly showed us where we were going to move. Often Mom packed the five kids off to the library to check out books about the new place. Every move seemed like an exciting adventure that we all looked forward to. Of all the preparations, though, the most important to my parents was to locate the Mormons in this new place and wherever we moved, we were in church the first Sunday. Church. A familiar-looking place, rituals we knew, hymns we sang by heart, language we understood, concepts that were familiar and comforting, our culture, our home. And instant friends who were often not only part of the Mormon community but the military community as well.

We lived on a very charged island of Guam in the late 1960s, where B-52 bombers moved twenty-four hours a day on their way to and from bombing raids over North Vietnam, even while there were still dangerously live World War II munitions to be careful of in the jungles. We were in Panama during the heated canal treaty talks of the mid-1970s, where regular student riots sometimes confined us to the Canal Zone or even to the Air Force base we lived on. There was an early 1980s Portugal that was struggling enough to receive U.S. foreign aid typically reserved for developing countries. I served a Mormon mission in Argentina during the last years of the 1970s, a troubled time when thousands were tortured and killed by corrupt generals who held power and where closet Peronistas' undying devotion for Evita was quietly shared at risk of imprisonment. It was a time of helplessness and inhumanity when you could stand behind an Argentine police station, as I once did, and hear the screams of a man being tortured and your only sane choice was the insanity of walking away, as I did.

Throughout these landscapes in change and worlds in turmoil, the continuity and familiarity of the Mormon Church prevailed. My Mormon Church. I now understand it was my constant, it was my safe harbor. It was home. I didn't need to be from someplace, I was a Mormon.

COMMUNITY

It can be quite a journey to leave a community you helped build and that profoundly enriched you. For some people, such a journey is more consciously chosen than it is for others. For some, the destination is "anywhere but here" while for others it is intentionally unknown. For others still, it is the leaving that matters; the implication of destination or even just "noncommunity" does not yet register. Each of these partially describes my journey away from my Mormon community, which was, at first, physical, and eventually spiritual.

During my undergraduate work at Brigham Young University, I began to feel troubled by past Mormon Church doctrine that denied the priesthood to black men. I was increasingly concerned with what I perceived to be the diminished value of women. For the first time in my life, I understood Mormon culture was not equal to Mormon doctrine—a significant distinction I hadn't previously understood.

In the Mormon Church, you learn to accept the words of church leaders. I now wanted to challenge and debate church issues, and I looked for someone to give me that permission. It was, for this Mormon-schooled young man, an enormous, almost unspeakable thing when I decided to give *myself* permission to disagree with the church.

After graduating from Brigham Young University, I moved to Washington, DC. There, I continued to be involved in the church, but with a changed mind-set in which I enjoyed frequent discussion and debate of church policy and culture with open-minded, and to me, very interesting Mormon friends. By the time I began dealing with being gay, I was thirty years old. Although I continued to believe in my Mormon God, I was already less involved with the local congregation and more in charge of determining which church teachings were helpful tools in my life.

I cannot say there were dramatic shifts in my Mormon Church experience when I finally understood and embraced that I was gay. I also cannot minimize the significance of clearing the Mormon hurdle—the final one in my coming out—but at the time I didn't think about breaking with the church. What felt appropriate, instead, was to recognize homosexuality as simply another area where I felt the church was wrong. I saw the church had adopted different policies on homosexuality over the years, policies that seemed to trail society's views. I remember writing in my journal my personal belief that church leaders didn't yet have homosexuality figured out and when they got it right, I would listen. In the meantime, I would follow my heart and not join the many victims of the church's mishandling of, as church leaders put it, "those with homosexual problems." (Interestingly, the word "homosexual" is officially used by the Mormon Church as an adjective, never a noun.)

At that point in my life, I was in my early thirties and was established in Washington, DC, with wonderful friends and an active life. I was happily engaged in my chosen profession. Coming out had been the painful journey it often is. Looking back, I was amazed and sobered at what I had managed, and I was proud of myself. Gay men and lesbians were an endless source of fascination. I found commonality in their lives and stories and felt a strong sense that I was entering a new community of which I was a part. Finally, there was the comfort I felt in my spirituality, even as I recognized its diminished Mormon focus. All of this helped define my changed sense of spiritual, emotional, and physical community. But spiritual journeys I thought had wound down were not yet over. I was going to discover that the experience of community with gay men that I imagined, was to be something different.

Throughout the rest of my thirties, I experienced profound spiritual change. Whereas I had already journeyed away from my Mormon *community,* I was to travel farther still from my Mormon *spirituality.* The journey was gradual but explicit and never boring. Certain events were catalytic, in particular the accidental death of a friend in eastern Hungary that left me cold. Interestingly, I didn't wonder where Lester was as a person or a soul but I deeply felt other unanswered questions. Where was the dance in Lester's eyes? Where did that go? Where was the spark that ignited his smile? Where were Lester's bounce and his joy? Where were these things that found expression through Lester? Where did all of that go? My spiritual journey led me to ask these kinds of questions and eventually led me to satisfying answers. That experience fed into my discovery that being gay was not necessarily the spiritual gift I earlier believed it to be any more than is being straight or a bird or a rock. My sexuality and spiritually disconnected and eventually reconnected in new ways. This was a rich and active period of letting go, redefining, discovery, and expansion. My spiritual life and perspective today are far removed from that of my youth, and I cherish the present as I do the past.

Playing out against the backdrop of my spiritual journey was my experience of discovering community with gay men. I was a newly self-identified gay man at age thirty-one and by then was long at ease making small talk with strangers at cocktail parties, developing friendships, or even just sharing a joke to ease tension while waiting in line at the Department of Motor Vehicles. Social tools that I wielded with ease felt unexpectedly cumbersome in my contact with gay men with whom I found signals, symbols, and organizations of meaning that confused me and felt less embracing than what I expected.

It was after a visit to a Names Project Quilt display that I began to revise my expectations of community in the gay community. With the exception of the first display, I have seen the full quilt each time it has been in Washington, DC, and find it a remarkable experience to be among the panels in their entirety. At the full display in 1996, I wandered alone, reading and experiencing individual panels. Through their quilts, I saw men who struck me as interesting or funny, and men with whom I felt a connection. So very, very often I found myself saying, "I would love to have known this person." After some time, several emotional hours, I was struck that many of these same men would have treated me like shit. This was immediately followed by the thundering realization that I felt a greater sense of community with dead gay men than live ones.

Still, today, I move with greater ease in a room of straight people I don't know than in a room of gay men I don't know. By far, my experience with nongay people has felt positive and affirming. Paradoxically, the only consistent source of discrimination and rejection I have felt as a gay man, is from gay men.

Although there is *a* gay community, I feel there is little gay *community,* which, once I thought about it, made sense. Here is what I learned. In the United States, gay men and lesbians are likely too diverse and varied to impart the kind of embracing sense of community I enjoyed, and came to expect, as part of more homogenous groups such as the Mormons and the military, or as a student at a small college or a homeowner in a neighborhood. I came to understand that the experience of gay community is not so much ready-made for me to receive but is, instead, something for me to extend, to create. That experience can exist, then, through the gay community of one's own making, which in my life is a wonderful gift. I love these gay men and even though many of us are geographically dispersed, they are my community, my home. I imagine that if we get to grow old, we will walk that road together.

I notice that I can only truly reflect on my experience with community when I consider my life's journeys—the fixed intertwined with the transitory. A few years ago, I purchased a striking painting of a shrouded, travel-weary figure standing at what the composition suggests is the end of a long, even dark, journey. Immediately ahead is a vast sweep of blue sky, open air, and light. It was shortly after I had come out and I sat alone in a private room in the gallery and wept, for I felt I was looking at myself. The painting continues to be a visual metaphor of journeys since and a reassurance for my experience in journeys future.

MY FATHER

My father died last year, before my fortieth birthday. I was his third child and his first son. We tossed the ball in the backyard and talked about how an engine works as we leaned under the open hood of the family car. I hated playing ball and engines were boring. But even as young as I was, I sensed he initiated these activities because he was supposed to. And Dad was good at doing what he was supposed to. I was unaware that I didn't have to be good at playing ball nor did I have to be interested in engines so I went along, as he did. We were both doing what we thought we were supposed to do and I remember feeling awkward in these engagements. Dad must have sensed it even if he didn't understand it, just as I didn't understand it.

Dad had two sons after me who played in Little League and had paper routes. Those father-son interactions, so much more traditional, must have felt easier to him, even a relief. I wish I could ask him. I looked forward to asking him such things.

I grew up taking piano lessons and in high school had a hundred plants in my bedroom, many of them in macramé hangers that I made out of jute. This was, after all, California in the early 1970s! I was entering my teen years and instead of rock concerts, I went to musicals in San Francisco. Everybody loved Neil Young, but John Denver was my favorite. I played my two Lily Tomlin comedy albums so many times I wore them out. I didn't fit the typical son role, and I think this was mildly confusing to my dad. Our relationship did not express what he probably expected would result from his dutiful and ongoing fatherly deeds. Sometimes I felt awkward or uncomfortable around him. At the same time, I don't remember him not being proud of me or not supporting me. Even as he perhaps didn't understand what motivated me, I always knew he was my father and that he loved me.

When I was in my twenties, Dad reflected on raising his five kids. He said with a bit of wonder, as if he had recently come to understand, that people don't always fit into a mold and where one child is good at football another child is good at playing the piano and it's all good. Or am I imagining that he said that? But I think he did.

When I was still a kid in the 1960s, there was a TV show called *My Three Sons* that starred Fred MacMurray. My dad sort of looked like him and, of course, he had three sons. We watched that show every week; my brothers and I piled into our dad's arms in his bed. As the show started, we moved our feet in time with the music just like the cartoon of the moving feet in the show's introduction. And every time Dad would mimic the show's narrator to say, "My three sons." We got a kick out of that.

I grew up hearing my father tell stories of the years he lived in Argentina as a Mormon missionary. He had tango records and gaucho souvenirs, and he taught us to count to ten and sing children's songs in Spanish. When you go on a Mormon mission, you don't select your location. At age nineteen, I opened the envelope to see where I was to be sent; I couldn't believe it was to Argentina. I was thrilled and Dad was proud. Parents are discouraged from visiting children who are serving missions, but Dad was given permission and surprised me. When I first saw him and fell into his arms, he cried. It was the only time I saw my father cry. He was proud that his son was a missionary and I was proud to work where he had been twenty-five years prior.

Over time, my brothers and sisters and I left home to make our own lives in different parts of the country and the globe. I don't know about my parents but I certainly took for granted that we would all be around awhile. As I moved through my twenties and thirties, this was all the more important because my perceptions of my parents changed and there were things I wanted to talk to them about, questions I wanted to ask. And of course, there was the issue of my being gay. I came out to my parents in a long and carefully written letter in 1993. A couple of months later, my work sent me to live in Eastern Europe and two months after that, my parents moved overseas to be Mormon missionaries, an assignment that extended to four years. They worked constantly and didn't have time to fully process the news I gave them in 1993, the news my mother initially described as "devastating."

I so looked forward to their return. I looked forward to being available to walk that road with them, the road many parents walk when they learn a child is gay. I looked forward to their return for a million other reasons as well. I wanted to reconnect with my dad. Through the years, I believed I understood him better. I understood his was a black-and-white world, a quality that allowed him to excel as a soldier and as a Mormon whereas my world of the many shades of gray put me on other paths. People admired my father and I wanted to explore that and countless other things. Surely he had reflections of his own to share as he approached seventy years of age.

He and my mother got on the airplane to come home after completing their missionary service and during the flight he collapsed. He had advanced prostate cancer and would die ten months later. I put things on hold and moved to California shortly after his diagnosis. I was selfish. I wanted time with my dad that I knew I couldn't have again. If I didn't do it, I would live forever knowing I could have.

* * *

It was around midnight and Mom had already gone to bed. My dad slept in the hospital bed in his study where I had just finished checking my e-mail. I sat down next to him, held his hand, and put my other hand on his chest. I talked to him about his life, his family, the roles he played, the duties he carried out, and his service to others. I wanted him to hear he was a remarkable man and he was loved. I spoke quietly to him and after about half an hour, his mouth formed unspoken words and then he simply stopped breathing.

When I was in my twenties, I saw a graphic documentary about a family that could not take care of its aging father. The documentary left me unsettled and disturbed and I immediately called my dad in California. Through my tears, I told him if he ever got old and couldn't take care of himself, I would take care of him. I explained that I had just seen an upsetting documentary and I think he got a kick out of the whole thing. With a chuckle he said he sure appreciated the offer and would keep it in mind. Then we both had a laugh.

It is a funny thing that on paper words are black and white, but if you chose the right ones and in a certain order, they leave colors and feelings in their wake. Can I, or anyone, piece together words that tell what those final months with my father mean? Maybe, if words were huge and detailed holographic images, each a harried concoction of sound and color and able to whip into your life to make you feel things beyond the reach of rational explanation. Maybe then I could choose a string of words that would make you, or me, understand the ways that experience was spiritual, complex, and still too intimate for me to contemplate at length.

In the early 1970s, my dad was called up to serve a tour of duty in the Vietnam War. I was in my early teens. Before he left, he took my two brothers and me camping in Northern California. Years later, I realized he was giving his children final memories of moments with him in case he did not return.

When Mormons die, they are dressed for burial in ritual clothing. With a broken heart, I asked my mother if my two brothers and I could dress Dad and asked my brothers if they would join me. The morning of the funeral, my brothers and I drove to the mortuary to be ushered into a small room where my dad was. I asked my brothers to remember that twenty-five years prior Dad had taken us camping to give us one last memory together in case he didn't come back from Vietnam. This time he wasn't coming back and dressing him in the ritual clothing would be the final memory, our one last moment together. In an ironic postscript, we learned my dad's cancer was likely related to exposure to Agent Orange during his service in Vietnam. We had always been thankful Dad returned safe from the war, but I guess he didn't.

What did I lose when I lost my dad? When he died, there wasn't great depth to our relationship because for several years we had not been a part of each other's daily life. My heart broke for the future I won't have with my dad, the relationship I so looked forward to building. That was a terrible, terrible thing for me to accept. I didn't get to ask my dad the questions I wanted to. We never got to walk the roads together I thought we might, as two men. He gave me so much, and yet we are so different. I got to have him for the time that I had him. He didn't die alone; he died hearing words of love. He loved his children.

FORTY

I don't think there is anything magical or noble about being forty. But what I know is that just like there are no shortcuts to a five-mile run, there are no shortcuts to age forty. Of course that is true of any age, but for some unknown reason only now am I high enough up a mountain to see a view that surprises me with its meaning. I look back and there is a life that is now long enough to have seen cycles, completions, and beginnings; stretches of life journeys; experiences and understandings. In an unexpected way I feel I'm earning my stripes; I'm gaining wisdom. There is also a sense of just getting started and of feeling all the more equipped for what is ahead. I didn't think about how forty would feel, but it feels good, like a badge of honor.

When I woke up on the day I turned forty, I had an unanticipated and never-before-contemplated response. I thought to myself, "I'm forty, and I'm still here." I'm still here. A good many gay men born in 1958 are not here; they didn't make it to forty and I did. It is as if I have thus far survived a place, in this case a time, that claims people, that doesn't let them continue. I know I'm not home free but part of me feels like it, or that I've at least gotten pretty far. How odd it is to me that on some level, I must have expected that I wouldn't make it to forty or that I just wouldn't make it. Turning forty reminded me that I'm still here. I'm still here and I like the look of things.

Chapter 15

A Photograph

Mark M. Harris

I have a photograph of my father that appears quite old now, as if it was taken in a different place in a different time. Perhaps it was. In the photograph, my father is seated with another man at dinner in a restaurant. My mother tells me that it is the Palmer House in Chicago, and that the other man in the picture was a business associate of my father's. Although the table is relatively small, they are seated side by side, in the manner of intimates. My father appears to be at this time somewhat younger than my current forty years. The other man is attractive, as is my father. My father is holding his fork with his pinkie finger extended in the way of royalty, or perhaps of a man with a certain sensibility. The other man is smiling, somewhat shyly. At first glance, they could be mistaken for lovers sharing a quiet evening or perhaps celebrating a special occasion. These, however, are not ideas that I would discuss with my mother.

My earliest awareness of being different came when I was in first grade. I had my first crush. It was on Astro Boy, the young hero of a Japanese cartoon that had somehow made its way onto television in Iowa. Astro Boy was confident, outgoing, cheerful, and popular. He also was cute, wearing what looked like a little black swimsuit and having a cape that allowed him to fly. Two booster rockets occupied that place where his feet would be. About that time, I also developed a crush on my first real live boy. Steve was a lot like Astroboy, at least in my mind. Although he had traditional feet and tennis shoes instead of rockets, everything else about him was pretty much the same. I felt as if he was my hero, sent to rescue me from enemies I only sensed, but did not yet understand. I would sit on the sidelines while he played boy games of dodgeball and red rover, admiring his athletic prowess and the way that he carried himself, and the special interest that he took in me.

Sometime in junior high, I began an important phase of growing up. Through a neighbor who was a police officer, I joined the local Police Explorer Scouts post. Dan, the police officer, was gruff, self-assured, bright, and very funny. I was a gangly and awkward teen when I put on the blue uniform of the post. I can only imagine how ridiculous I looked. This was one of my first indoctrinations into what it meant to be a man. I spent many nights through junior high school and high school riding in a patrol car late into the night. On weekends, there would be activities such as weapons training and directing traffic for special events. This is also where I learned to drink coffee, and to drink it black. The officers said that if I was going to ride with them, that I would need to drink what they drank.

High school for me was a mixed experience. I was in the school band, playing the drums, and also in a high school rock band. We called ourselves "Aurora Borealis" and played mostly covers of popular songs by bands such as Deep Purple and Kiss. At the same time, I continued in the police post. I think that I was searching for a place to belong. I had good friends, but was also harassed at school for my participation in the Police Scouts. This was my first experience of being openly hated by other people. This was also my first experience of life not being "fair." The reality was that as a Scout, I was often in the position of being able to help someone get a break when they deserved one by persuading officers to go easy on people. Despite this, the taunting continued.

High school also brought the developing awareness of my sexual attraction to other guys. I noticed all the cute boys that I went to school with. It amazes me to this day how little snippets of memory are seared into my consciousness. Like the time that I saw my friend Scott in the showers after gym; I was amazed at the perfection of his gymnast's body. I remember as well watching my friend John changing clothes in his room, unaware of the effect that it was having on me as I took in the contrast of his tan and hairy legs against his white underwear. Or the many memories of guys in short cut-off jeans that were way too tight. I still regret that tight cut-offs and Speedos have never come back into fashion.

When I went to college, I began slowly to deal more directly with my sexual orientation. I went to Iowa State University in Ames to major in psychology. While in college, I developed the identity of a partier. As a high school student, I had done my share of drinking. Back then, you could legally buy alcohol at the age of eighteen. Before that, friends were always available to buy us beer. In college I was also introduced to smoking pot. As a Police Scout, I had bought into the distinction that alcohol was OK, but that pot was evil. I learned otherwise when friends persuaded me to give pot a try. I found that pot really relaxed me and decreased the anxiety that I felt in social situations.

I made some of my best friends in college. They are all straight guys, most of whom I met either in the residence halls or in classes. It was one of the first times in my life that I felt I belonged, that I was "one of the guys." My closest friend was Rich. I had a big crush on him. He embodied all the things that I felt were lacking in myself. He was attractive, confident, outgoing, and had a deep tan and great legs. I fell in love. Spending time with him was both excruciating and wonderful. By my senior year, I had taken an apartment off campus with some of these friends. As most of our group still lived in the residence halls, my apartment became the gathering place. Most nights we would stay up until 3:00 or 4:00 playing cards, drinking, and listening to music. As it was too late for anyone to try to go home, most of the guys just crashed there. Rich would always crash in my room, sharing my bed. I had to develop a lot of self-control, lying there watching him sleep next to me in the darkness.

In the middle of my senior year, my father died. A lifelong smoker, he developed lung cancer at the age of fifty-seven. In an effort to "protect" me, my family did not tell me the true diagnosis or prognosis until it was too late. By the time that I was at home for Christmas vacation, my father was in decline. The day that he died, he told me that he was having trouble breathing and needed to go to the hospital. Not knowing how serious his condition was, I argued with him, afraid of what his going to the hospital might mean. Finally he convinced me, and we called for an ambulance. My father requested that they not run their lights or sirens coming to our house, as he did not want to make a scene for the neighbors. The ambulance quietly pulled into our driveway, and the EMTs came up the narrow stairway leading to our upstairs where my father lay in pain. Unable to get a stretcher through the opening, they gathered my 6' 4" father in their arms and carried him downstairs like a child. I had never seen him looking so small. My father passed away later that night, the day before Christmas, with all of us gathered around him.

The shock of my father's death, as well as the growing acknowledgement that I was gay, propelled me to start coming out to my family and friends. I had been in a gay support group at the university (telling my friends that I was going to a class at that hour) and was beginning to feel more settled with the idea that I was gay, and that it was not going to change. I started by telling my friends one by one, starting with Rich. He was completely surprised. After some initial hesitation (after all, he had not ever known a gay person that he was aware of, let alone one that was a close friend) he became very supportive. One by one, I told the rest of my friends. They were all surprised as well. I guess that I had done a good job of hiding. The atmosphere was a little strained in the apartment for the first few weeks, and I am sure that many late-night conversations about my being gay took place among them. Finally I knew that I was accepted when they started kidding me about it. They would see an unattractive woman on television and kid each other about who should be with her. When an unattractive man would appear, they would say "And there is one for Mark, too." I knew then that things were okay.

Being able to be myself around my friends was the best feeling in the world. The laughing and kidding continued. I celebrated a birthday around that time, and Rich and another friend Scott asked me what I wanted to do. Pausing briefly, I said that I wanted to go to Des Moines, about thirty miles away, and go to my first gay bar. They both thought that would be a great idea. These two very straight guys, in the early 1980s in Iowa, decided on their own that they would tell anyone that hit on either of them that they were a couple. That night was a blur. I remember that we all danced together and had many laughs.

Being gay at that time and place also led to some other strange scenes. When gathered around other male friends that did not know about my being gay, Rich would always laugh uncontrollably when any of them would change clothes in front of me, or stand there naked ready to get dressed after a shower as I looked on. They never did understand what he thought was so funny. I remember as well when I started to date. None of us were all that active in dating, so it was the source of a lot of kidding and being given a hard time when any of us actually had a date. I had met a guy at the local Unitarian Church and he asked me out for dinner. We arranged that he would pick me up at the apartment and we would go from there.

When Rich and the other guys found out about this they were insistent that he come into the apartment to get me, and that he would need to "pass inspection" before they would let me go out with him. It made quite a sight for him to walk into the apartment and see my friends all lined up sitting on the sofa, asking him questions about himself and his intentions toward me.

I also came out to my mother at this time. Buoyed by the success that I had had talking to my friends, I told my mom that we needed to talk. I was home from college for the weekend and invited her out to the porch for a talk. She asked if she should make a drink. I suggested that she make two. Before we even sat down, she said, "I think I know what it is. You are going to marry Judy, aren't you?" Judy was the woman that I had dated throughout high school and college. I was surprised (having read somewhere that mothers usually already sensed things about their sons) and replied, "No, I am not going to marry Judy, and probably not anyone else. I am gay." After a long sip of her drink, she paused and said that she was surprised and not sure how she felt about that. Then and now a devout Roman Catholic, she was struggling. She did make it clear that she didn't want me to ever bring anyone home, and that she didn't want to know any of the details.

After college, I was accepted for graduate study in psychology at Ohio State University. I eagerly accepted their offer of full funding and headed east to Ohio. That began one of the best periods of my life. Graduate school was wonderful. I was in a respected program, everyone was warm and supportive, and I started the experience as an out gay man. I had no problems at all in this with either the faculty or the other students. I also took advantage of the active gay social scene in Columbus, and went through my period of "running the bars" and making up for the sex that I did not have growing up in Iowa. I also grew more confident and began to work out and look better. I had, as many of us do, such a traumatic experience in PE classes growing up that I assumed that physical fitness was something for others. The attention that I began to get was nice, particularly after all the years of low self-esteem and self-doubt.

At age thirty-two, long after I had given up hope of finding a decent relationship, I met Brian. Brian had recently moved to Columbus, where I was now working as a psychologist. We had already spotted each other at various social occasions when he came to an open house that my roommates at the time and I were having for our new apartment. As the last guests were making their way down the front stairway to leave, Brian turned instead into the kitchen to rinse out a few dishes. By the time he returned to the living room, the lights were dimmed, the candles lit, and soft music was playing in the background. That was our first date. Seven years later, we are still on that date.

Being gay at midlife for me means a lot of things, all of them good. Gone are the emotional storms and self-doubts of the first four decades of my life. Life is a lot smoother sailing now. I know that gay relationships can succeed because I am in one that is succeeding.

I credit a lot of that to my partner Brian's patience and unfailing love for me. Or, as my mother (who has come around somewhat since those early years) put it, "If you have to be with a man, I am glad that you are with someone like Brian." Both Brian and I realized from the beginning that it is more work to be in a relationship than it is to be single. That helped us to lay a lot of groundwork that still supports the relationship today. We did more talking about things in the first six months than many people do in a lifetime. I think that this factor, as well as loving each other and having realistic expectations about a relationship, has helped us.

The other nice thing about being at this point in life for me is to have many good friends that I have now known for decades. Most of my closest friends are still, and have always been, my straight male friends from school. This may be a bit unusual for a gay man, but it has been my experience from the beginning. I have stood up at the weddings of most of my friends, and Brian and I together are a part of their lives. Both Rich and Scott have given me the honor of being a godparent to one of their children. These children are growing up thinking nothing is unusual about having an Uncle Brian and Uncle Mark that are together. Brian and I are now settled in the Iowa City,

Iowa, area, and life has calmed down enough that we are beginning to discuss our commitment ceremony. I know that many of the people that have loved us along the way will be part of that day as well.

I wouldn't want to be any other age, at any other place, and with anyone else than I am right now. I feel very blessed to be able to say that. Part of reaching this point in life for me is having few regrets about the past, and few real fears about the future. I think that this has come to me only with age and experience. Brian and I live in a small college town in eastern Iowa, but you can routinely see gay male couples, lesbian couples, mixed race couples and, in general, people of all varieties getting along. We have been welcomed into our middle-class neighborhood with genuine warmth and friendship. We hope to share by example some of what being gay has taught us—that landscaping is good, fabric is fun, and that not every house on the block need look alike.

I look now at that photograph of my father at the Palmer House and wonder for the hundredth time who he was. Did he know? Was he allowed to know? Did he lead the life that he wanted to lead? These are things that I will never know. Being gay for me at midlife means getting to know who I am, getting to construct the life that I want and to share it with those I love. It means getting to be part of what a client once described to me as "this great secret club," with members everywhere, that not everyone is lucky enough to get the chance to join.

Chapter 16

Between the Living and the Leaving

Armand R. Cerbone

GETTING READY

Everybody has their story,
but the stories are really the same story.

Edward Ball, *Slaves in the Family*[1]

If I am going to write about being gay at middle age, then I am going to write about sex, love, and aging. For most people, these experiences will shape character. Certainly, no one, except those who die young, escapes aging. But for gays, who live in a society troubled by their affections, sex and love and growing older do more than shape character; they are crucibles that test the soul. This has been very true in my life. I do not regret or bemoan that in any way. For in braving the test, I have had as much love, success, and happiness in my life as pain, fear, and anguish. From it I have squeezed a measure of wisdom and understanding. For these reasons, I think the scars gay people bear, often with anger and protest but as often with camp humor, have much to say to the world that this world needs to hear.

I see middle age as a paradoxical time that swings equally in two directions, forward and back. Sufficient years have passed from which to glean some wisdom and plenty of years remain to make good use of that wisdom. I have spent some of these middle years groping more or less blindly to find myself, to see more clearly who I am. Ultimately, I have enjoyed a measure of success and happiness, if those mean having love in one's life and a career one loves. But I would not have these things were it not for other men and women before me who fought for a gay place in the sun. I am happy to be in their very great debt. They are my spiritual parents.

As a pre-television child, I lived in movie houses sheltering myself from the frightening punishments a little queer boy would suffer on the straight streets of midcentury Boston. I sat every Saturday and Sunday in the dark, safe, watching lives unfold as I thought they should. Every problem was resolved, every threat nullified. In the best of these films it was all accomplished with song and dance. Movie life was more than a dream for me. It was a promise I believed in. Movies kept alive a hope that someday even my life would be full and free from fear. Only with the hindsight of therapy and gay film criticism have I appreciated the irony that what made me feel safe also reinforced a heterosexual dream that made real life a nightmare. Those movies of my childhood were seductive diversions, reel life for real life. They kept me captive in a sly lie, believing that I could only be real if I lived and proselytized the straight (and white male) life.

I was also Catholic—very Catholic. I spent four years in a seminary preparing to be a priest. Again with hindsight I can see that like the movies, this too was a flight from the angst of real life into an idealized role. If the celibate priesthood was essentially a role in which I could bury my sexual self, then the Catholic orthodoxy of self-denial was the armor that insured salvation and sanctity. The civil rights movements of the 1960s and the *aggiornamento* of Pope John XXIII's Vatican Council turned my world on its head. Where there had been only a docile "yes" to others and "no" to self, there was a liberating "yes" to self and a cathartic "no" to others. Roles and rules I thought written in stone fractured—not all at once but inexorably, like an egg hatching. Then came Stonewall. And with it challenges that shattered the supremacy and monopoly of heterosexuality.

I was unaware of the reports that gays in Greenwich Village had risen up against the police raids on their sanctuaries. I was aware only that Judy Garland, whose screen life animated my weekend matinees, had died. My dreams for freedom ignited later with the marches for gay pride that commemorated that turning point. I gorged myself on gay-themed books and newspapers that multiplied in bookstores like Catholics in Boston. When I saw the first gay bar on Halsted Street in

Chicago install clear windows open to the streets, I got a rush like no other. That simple, quiet change—more than any other for me—signaled an end to hiding and the beginning of a life as normal and frank as the straights around me enjoyed. As much as any march it said we were here to stay. The conclusive turn of the key in my closet door came when as a new graduate in 1973, I saw fellow psychologists sit in a hotel room in Montreal to create the Association of Gay Psychologists. Fourteen years later, I would chair that organization.

It took decades before I could look upon my queer face in the mirror with a sincerely happy smile. But once I accepted being gay as normal, as normal as twins are normal and odd only in their frequency, the terrain of human sexuality became a new landscape. The simple fact that I existed as a homosexual demanded I rethink the nature, meanings, and norms of human sexuality. Heterosexuality could no longer be the monolithic norm of human sexuality. No more forcing facts into categories that twisted reality. In this new world, the facts themselves determined the categories. No other explanation, justification, or correction was necessary. Homosexuals are. Enough said.

If my fifty-eight years have taught me anything, it has been the benefit of coming out. From the day I vowed never to feel bad about being gay, my life has moved toward happiness, better relationships, and even greater professional success. That day was more than thirty-five years in the making. It came in a moment of self-realization late in 1978 as I boarded a TWA flight back from Los Angeles. I had spent a week in Los Angeles as the guest of a man who became a very special mentor and friend. He had been kind and nurturing to me, introduced me to several gay and lesbian luminaries I had read about and admired, and immersed me in a gay subculture that exhilarated me with its richness and variety. The freedom of expression and behavior I enjoyed in L.A. contrasted loudly with the constrained silence of my more closeted life in Chicago. When my friend leaned over to kiss me goodbye at the airport, I turned away anxious that someone should see and *know*. Boarding the plane, I felt shame. My denial of that kiss betrayed all that I had been shown and given. As the plane climbed toward Chicago and home, I grew angry, very angry. I vowed never again to deny the truth of who I am or deny any love shown me. No more would I sacrifice any of my life or happiness on the altar of heterosexual hegemony. For what, I asked myself? To perpetuate the myth that people like me are defective and deficient? For whom? For people so afraid of truth they would rather believe we don't exist. Or worse, for people who would imprison, maim, or kill men like me to maintain their fictions? That moment, as much as any other, has brought me to these pages. And it is that conversion that informs much of what you will read here.

AGING

> *. . . the virtues of aging include both the blessings*
> *that come to us as we grow older*
> *and what we have to offer*
> *that might be beneficial to others.*

Jimmy Carter, *The Virtues of Aging*[2]

I am fifty-eight. It's a very paradoxical time. I am not old, but very definitely not young. Beyond even my middle years, but not yet in my golden years. I am old enough to know who I am and to like that person, but unfinished enough to be still working through issues from my childhood. No longer affected by the panic attacks of my forties, but still vulnerable to self-doubt when fears of abandonment shake my world. Even as I take pride in living my sexuality out loud, I can catch myself freezing in fear at a homophobic remark made in the company of civil or uncivil folk. At fifty-eight, I sometimes resent the costs sustained in living gay in a hostile culture—like never having children, like leaving my family in Boston for Chicago so I could come out. Far safer to come out as an émigré, unencumbered by reputation and history as a heterosexual. Much less explaining to do, less need to defend, less risk in exploring the forbidden and the taboo. Freer to experiment with sex and play with identity as I dared not attempt in adolescence. I also resent being absent during my niece and nephew's growing years, missing years of family holidays, daily dinners, quotidian trials and joys that glue loved ones together. I resent losing straight friends when I fled their world into the gay demimonde. I left them with unanswered questions because I couldn't fully function in divergent worlds.

I resent that hiding from friends and family froze their understanding of me in the 1960s. To them I remained the troubled naif who left for graduate school in the Midwest—green and idealistic. It helps explain the shock they tried to mask when I returned home ten years later with a gay lover in tow. That I would expect their embraces instead of their uneasiness reveals how little I understood the magnitude of the changes I had made. That I would be angry at their stumbling and resistance reveals how little I reckoned the years it took to evolve, years of cocooning out of sight till I could hatch transformed, mature and sure of my new wings. I also failed to recognize the challenge my coming out presented to the treasured myth that our family was better than others, closer and more loving, special and exemplary.

I resent that my body was another casualty of the closet. I feared the betrayal my body presented. I feared what its failure to respond to the allures of women might reveal. I feared the betrayal my eyes might give when they looked on another man. Fearing the betrayal, I rejected the body altogether. Fearing the consequences of my sexual desire, I rejected sex altogether. Coming out set the stage for a reclamation and development of my body that was stunning to me. As I came out, I lived more in my body. I remember the first night I slept naked in my graduate dormitory bed; I was thirty. I thrilled with the sensuality of sheets against my exposed skin. At thirty-two, I began working out. I was surprised with the slendering of waist, the hardening of muscles, the rise of pectorals and biceps. I was dismayed and delighted by the random whistle I would get from other gay men.

I remember catching my reflection after showering one summer afternoon in my fortieth year. This tanned body, trim and tight, was mine. I recognized it as the kind of body I had so often lusted after with guilt and worry. It unnerved me to acknowledge what I found handsome and sexy. But it was more relief than pride that prompted my thanking God for that moment. I could always look back, I thought, in the knowledge that, despite whatever ravages time might work on my body, there had been this moment when I knew I had the kind of body I had always wanted. I luxuriated in the obvious narcissism of the moment as an achievement of the spirit as much as body. For me it was a triumph over homophobia, for this was a body developed to attract other gay men, not to attract a woman with whom to procreate.

Accepting sex and sensuality marked the end of those very troubled years during which I felt stunted within the constraints of affected heterosexuality. But doing so led to another surprise. I liked sports. Well, at least some. Things physical, all sports and displays of strength, I had thought belonged exclusively to straight boys. Now I exulted in the things that *my* body could do. Joining my first gym laid nervous claim to a male province that had been strictly off limits to me. This man who hated snow learned to ski at fifty-three. This man who feared loss of control, any control, learned to careen on roller blades. This man who trembled at competitive sports relished winning a volleyball game and beating out my friends in Chicago's Proud to Run race. Last summer this man realized a childhood dream by swimming like Cousteau with sea turtles, eels, and octopuses. These achievements of the body redefined my sense of being a man; I feel as sure of my masculinity as any other man might and I can participate in the world of men *to the extent I wish* without that old fear of humiliating failure.

As a result, aging has been redefined, too. Until I embraced my sexuality, I tried to grow into life leaving sex behind. My development was lopsided, lagging behind my peers in some ways, outstripping them in others. I could never achieve that measure of comfort with and command of sexuality that marks a mature adult. In addition, anxiety about sexuality was constricting. I would orchestrate a sexless intimacy with women that frustrated and confused them and a sexually charged intimacy with men that attracted and alarmed them. Intellect, compassion, and emotional agility grew but interpersonal honesty and comfort suffered. Fear of homosexuality kept me in fear of myself and I lived half a life at best. I was a house divided, never completely safe, never completely sound. Coming out staged my recovery from fear. Today I am more in love with life than ever, less fearful and more willing to take risks.

No urban gay my age is a stranger to death. We all witnessed wave after wave of friends and friends of friends crash on the shoals of AIDS. We also witnessed the random and heinous slaughters of gay brothers and sisters. Always the untimeliness or the unfairness of those deaths made death a force to fight. Clinging to life was to fight against injustice, to fight against what was but need not be. The marks AIDS has left are not readily visible. They are there, however. I know I got tired, soul tired. I was luckier than most; AIDS got no closer than two or three close friends. But I lost count of the clients I lost. The deaths were too many to allow for grieving. I stopped going to memorials. I could hold a hand till the last breath but could not accompany the body to its grave.

Now I find myself surviving that wave to face another. Uncles, aunts, and friends of my parents have shriveled and are dying en masse. My mother's turn came last month. After the doctors left us with their diagnosis of cancer, I promised her that I would help her die and in return she would teach me how to die. I was not disappointed. I learned that dying is simply the last thing one does in living. She simply relaxed and let her presence recede. Some asked where I got the strength to watch while cancer withered her. Their questions led me to understand something else. I had been through this many times before. But always those deaths were untimely or violent. This death was peaceful, a last embrace of life. No unnatural wresting of life but a yielding to nature itself. Losing my mother hurt, but her death gave a healing that many others could not. It gave me a death to hope for. This death was intimate, shared with loved ones. It showed me that, like hers, mine could be the last act of living. That, given the chance, I could let go of life when it was time. That, if timely, it would feel good to do so. It helps with the fear of letting go and leaving all I know and love.

SEX

Let's talk about sex.

Madonna

I don't think we know that much about sex. I mean the kind of knowing that science gives us about our physical world. Not enough time and resources have been given to the empirical study of sexuality to answer our questions or hunches—a stunning fact in itself, given the pervasiveness and centrality of sex to the human experience. I understand this to be one more sorry result of the taboos against knowing our sexual selves. Nonetheless, a lack of knowledge has not kept us from making all sorts of pronouncements about sex and its place in human conduct. It is as though the pervasiveness of sex alone qualified some among us to decide for us all how sexuality should be managed. A dangerous limb to be out on. History has proven that relying on experience alone is quite precarious. Think of all the people vilified or worse for suggesting the world was round or, perish the thought, was not the center of the universe. Neither persistence nor broad consensus for a notion are adequate proofs of validity. I am reminded of Lily Tomlin's psychotic Bag Lady who theorized that reality is a collective hunch.

That being said, I will share my hunches about sex. Well, more about sex in my life. And particularly in my late middle years. For the need for sex and its meanings for me have decidedly changed from my youth and from my coming-out years. And I expect them to change further. But, at least in my life, letting go of cherished beliefs has demanded tolerance for ambiguity. I still need to know, but I don't need to be as sure as I used to. It was not easy getting here. For years following my coming out I suffered immobilizing panic attacks. And I still have much more to work through. I used to believe that closed relationships were better than open ones. Although I know this is still true for my relationships, I accept that for others the opposite can be true. What makes the difference seems to be what one needs in order to maintain intimacy. For me, sexual exclusiveness makes it possible to tolerate the emotional vulnerability intimate relationships require. It seems to me that others who prefer open relationships need assurances of independence and self-determination that freedom to have sex with someone other than their primary partner provides. I still don't know for sure. There have not been empirical studies sufficient in number to hold to one side of the debate or another with any authority. It remains distressing, then, to read or hear wholesale assumptions being made about the nature of same-sex relationships or about gay men. How often have you heard, as I have, that gay men are inherently promiscuous? Or that gay relationships can't last? What distresses me most is that these arguments will come from gay men themselves. The same arguments about promiscuity are conveniently used to laud or condemn sexual activity, depending on the speaker.

In my own life, I have had three relationships of five years or more. Each of them was with men I genuinely loved, each of them with rewards and satisfactions as well as a good measure of trouble. In the first two, the troubles and frustrations were more than the relationship could endure. Accepting the impasse in each was painful. But each came to an end, not solely but in large measure because of changes in my sexuality. In the first, I was just coming out, unsure of my sexuality and myself. In the second, although I was comfortable with being gay, I felt uneasy with sex in an intimate relationship. It surprisingly aroused fears of shame, a fear that permeated other aspects of the relationship. In my present relationship, I enjoy a knowledge of myself that is more confident and reliable. I know who I am. I have been able to negotiate the vicissitudes of sexual need and desire more effectively. But more about that when I talk about love.

I have had both open and closed relationships in my life. The closed ones have worked better for me. Even when they weren't working well, having a closed relationship helped resolve our conflicts by keeping us working on them or revealed sooner those impasses that resulted in the need to part. In the open relationship, I found options for sex with others provided a reduction in tensions that allowed us to remain a couple longer and so sustain our love. But, in that relationship at least, it substituted one form of caring for another. Our decision to see others for sex supplanted, in ways I don't fully understand yet, our need to be honest with each other about our needs. Discussing disappointments in each other, particularly sexual frustrations, ran the risk of shaming or humiliating the other. The risk was in violating an implicit rule that we never be further shamed for seeking sex with men. The disappointments grew more bitter as we were unable to resolve them.

Over the years, the frequency of sex, choice of, and numbers of partners have changed. I have had a lot of sex. Some might say I have been promiscuous. I would say I have been satisfyingly active. That is not to say that I believe all my sexual activities were safe or healthy. They were not. I remain a chronic carrier of hepatitis B as a result of that period. Ironically, it was that infection in 1979 that alerted me to the dangers of disease and probably saved me from infection with HIV when it was making its way deep into an unsuspecting gay community. But the heightened sexual activity of those years from thirty to forty-five met very important needs. The first was to heal wounds left by gay stigma. The second was to develop a self-concept that allowed for being sexual at all, let alone gay. Remember, I had been a devout Catholic. Another was to correct beliefs that I was unattractive. A fourth was to reclaim my physical self.

There were other benefits. I believe that period was a second chance to accomplish an adolescent task of development: integrating sexuality and exploring forms of intimacy prior to establishing adult relationships. Given the virulence of the taboos against such explorations in my teens, I couldn't do this until I was an independent adult with adult prerogatives of self-determination. But being an adult, I had adult needs while at the same time I was compelled to complete an adolescent task. Any wonder my first relationship would have been a muddle? Also, coming out increased my self-confidence everywhere. My sense of purpose enlarged and gave political, social and spiritual meaning to everything I did. I ventured into the gay community, offering workshops on relationships and sexuality. I pursued with enthusiasm positions of leadership with gay service, political groups, and arts groups, believing I was furthering the revolution begun at Stonewall. The conviction that I am part of a larger revolution is still true today and contributes importantly to my sense of well-being and happiness.

Perhaps this is no clearer than in my relationships with family. My brother accepted me immediately and continued to foster my relationship with his children. My father was murdered many years before I came out, but he had been adamantly antigay. Despite the closeness of my relationship with my mother and the mutual support we had given each other through many adversities, she had major problems with my sexuality. It took five years of confrontations and threats to shut her out of my life before she said to me, "You are a rare and beautiful man." I have never forgotten that night. In saying so, she admitted that it was she who had the problem, not I. Since then, she has admitted that my father's distance from me was rooted in his disappointment that I was "not the macho son he wanted." Again, his problem, not mine. I know if he were alive today, we would fight it out till he also accepted me. To be fair, I understood that there was absolutely nothing in their experience or backgrounds to help them accept a gay son. But I was not about to let their ignorance excuse them. They had a responsibility to their child who needed loving parents, no matter what my age. And that responsibility dictated that they expand their understanding before rejecting their son. They had to decide which was the sin: homosexuality or rejecting their child.

Also, I knew beyond a doubt they loved me. But their love, particularly my father's, felt like money in the bank that can't be spent.

What good was it? I was paper rich only. Once my mother complained to my brother that I had brought shame on the family. My answer to that was to threaten to close a door on our relationship. I would not, I protested, stay in a relationship with someone who was ashamed of me. "If you do that," she agonized, "I would never be happy another day in my life." "Then choose," I told her. She did. But it took years. The Christmas before she died, my mother apologized and wondered why she had such a hard time with my being gay.

I was well into my forties before I was so "out" that there was no closet left to hide in. By that time, I was convinced that I did not have a problem with being gay. The culture had the problem. Whatever problems I faced in being gay were not of my making. They were problems cultural stigmatization had given me. I didn't make them, but I had to face them. Nor could I allow them to stand in my way of being happy. If it meant changing the world, then that is what I would do.

I also had to face some realities about my sexual behavior that were hard for me. After a reasonable period of exploring sex, I had to wonder what I was exploring in continuing to pursue sex so ardently. Getting another man's pants off raised more questions than it answered. I got a clue one day in the wet areas of a Chelsea gym. I watched a very attractive man cruise repeatedly without luck. I wanted him to cruise me. In the excitement of the moment, I thought all I wanted was sex. But eventually when he did turn his attentions to me, surprisingly I couldn't respond. If I was that driven to have sex, I must want something more than just sex. And if he was equally driven, then his interest wasn't in me at all. I was going to get nothing! The recognition was startling. I saw that I wanted more than another sexual exchange, that much of what I wanted I would never find in such exchanges alone. Such encounters. no longer met my needs. I concluded further that there was a lot more being exchanged than either of us was aware. Though our behavior seemed simple and straightforward, the motivations that brought us there had to be more complex. And those complexities were better managed with reflection. I had come to a time in which I needed to think and feel more and act less.

This seemed hardly politically correct to me. Questioning the value and legitimacy of free sex felt seditious in a community that had fought painful battles for freedom of sexual choice and expression. I feared expulsion to the margins of gaydom. I feared being lumped with antisex conservatives. Worse, as a psychotherapist, I feared my positions might negatively affect my work with struggling clients. In truth, I was not questioning free sex at all. I was arguing that the meanings and determinants of all sexual behavior were more complex than any encounter might suggest.

I have had this discussion with many gay men and psychotherapists. I have found little agreement among them. But the range of their opinions and the intensity of their arguments have confirmed in my mind that indeed sexual behavior is always complex. As a result, I want more empirical study of sexuality. Until the results of responsible research are available, only conjecture and opinion will abound, no matter how well reasoned.

I don't expect those answers in my lifetime, though I am cheered to see more funding for gay studies available. In the meantime, I rely on the rigors of logic and empirical investigation to guide my thinking and behavior. Practically, this means recognizing when I am making inferences that go beyond proven fact. It means accepting what I think as a working hypothesis that will be confirmed or disconfirmed as facts become available. It means treating theories about sex as working metaphors, not descriptions of reality. Paradoxically, these positions have relaxed the anxieties that had often paralyzed me because I knew less than I should know. It has further bolstered my tolerance for ambiguity. I hope this has made me more responsible, respectful, and fair.

LOVE

Love may be the only socially acceptable form of psychosis.

Attributed to Harry Stack Sullivan

I have never found loving or being loved easy. Love is exciting but it raises anxieties about loss, self-worth, hurt, and disappointment. I have had to learn to master anxiety in order to manage being in love and being loved by another. Though I did not realize it at the time, I have been fairly adept at hiding parts of myself from my lovers.

These were parts of myself that I couldn't see, or simply didn't want to, such as my desire to control the other person. Often they were needs I couldn't admit to or couldn't ask for such as more and better sex or more access to inner feelings. But always I have found my relationships a good mirror. Sooner or later in every relationship, I met up with myself, and always it meant having to change. If I wanted to keep my relationship, then I had to fix myself, repair or eliminate what my partner experienced as distancing. Prior to turning fifty, I pressed to change my partner, but never unreasonably. One might drink too much, another might be emotionally constricted, and one might philander, the other lie. Not one could dispute my objections. But being right and reasonable brought me in the end to an empty bed and watching television alone. Why?

Sometime in my midfifties, my present lover confronted me with my wish to humiliate those who hurt me. He had hurt me deeply. "You just want to vent your spleen," he said. I opened my mouth to retort, "Yes, I do. And why not? You've hurt me deeply." But I cut my response short, for in that instant I saw myself as my mother, reproaching my father's drinking, his hurtfulness, his irresponsibility. I saw, too, the uselessness of her moral manipulations, the futility of her desperate importuning, and I saw the futility of mine. Not only did my mother's complaints not change him, they in fact diminished the man she loved. My lover's confrontation compelled me to see what I had not seen. My moral rectitude, my legitimate claim to the moral and psychological high ground was a Pyrrhic victory. In doing so, I put greater distance between us. Furthermore, it added additional hurt. I wanted to hurt back but did not want to see myself as hurtful. I could leave, but I loved him and did not want to be alone yet again. I had to choose: learn to handle hurt differently or leave.

I was confounded. I could not accept or support what was wrong. I would then be colluding with or denying what was wrong. Future objections to any offense would have no credibility. I had to decide what I wanted. First, I wanted my self-esteem. That meant that what was wrong was still wrong. It also meant that what hurt still hurt. I needed acknowledgment of both to remain in the relationship. If I was not to be hurtful, then I had to learn to confront without self-righteousness, without shaming. I had seen my mother press for recognition of her injured feelings and withhold acceptance until she got it. I saw how that just brought her further injury and loss. I determined that, no matter how hurt I was, hurting back was not an option. Any hurt to my partner would have to result from his recognizing the effects of his own behavior. I also had to remember who I was, i.e., the man he fell in love with. I was still that man. I had better be that man now. He would have to decide for himself if he wanted that man enough to change. And so we both changed, to keep our love. And our love grew, too.

I learned that no matter how hurt I get I have no license to hurt back. I learned that if I am going to grow, to love cleaner and better, then I have to be responsible, fair, and forgiving. I learned that if I provide these things to my lover, I can ask for them and expect them. If I don't get them or if I get hurt again, I can consider leaving or redefine the conditions and parameters of our relationship. I learned different ways to handle being hurt. Without realizing it, I had modeled the way I dealt with hurt after my mother. She would cajole and chide, cry and anguish. From what I had seen of my father's behavior, she had every right to do so. But it took years for me to see the shaming hidden in her confrontations and even longer to see how the shaming distanced her from her husband. In diminishing the man she loved, she made it more difficult for him to love her as an equal. How does one reach up from moral depths to love as a peer? How does one climb into bed with an inferior? It was a powerful model that made her look good. But it skewed the power balance in the relationship. It is hard to recover from shame, and no one can shame like a lover. I had adopted a dark side of my mother's love. Armed in rectitude, I would unwittingly shame my lovers for their failings, their acting out, and their disappointments. With wit I outwitted. Time and again, each told me he could not find the words I was looking for. I just saw that as a clearer sanction for withdrawing in sadness and regret.

Just when I finally caught on is difficult to say. I do believe it has something to do with my lover's calling me on it. I had to confront him about a matter that had been driving us toward a crisis. My lover's distrust of my motives and his belief that my actions came more from a wish to humiliate him and to vent my spleen rather than from a desire to resolve the conflict required me to face deeper anxieties and anger as I realized that he was right. Checking the impulse to shame my lover precipitated a painful confrontation with my own demons. I recognized that until I understood this other hurt and anger I could not work on our conflict with clarity and fairness. It took weeks for me to understand the roots of the hurt as issuing from my father's abandoning me when I was a boy. Why my lover should have constellated that anxiety is not important here. I know the threat of losing him was part of it. But I recalled two dreams I had during the previous summer that pointed toward unfinished business with my father. In each I was making love with my partner. In one, my young father's head was on my lover's body. In the other, my lover's head was on my father's body. Recognizing how much I still feared my father's disappointment, and feeling helpless to change, it led to a further realization. I was not the little boy anymore. I would never be the son my father wanted, but I could be the man my lover fell in love with.

Eliminating self-defeating manipulations left me to trust my lover to fix in himself what needed fixing. I could wait and support as long as I could see the change in progress. It meant trusting him to choose change rather than loss of the relationship. It also meant learning to love him with an open hand and heart. It meant risking further hurt and loss as a probability but having the confidence that I could tolerate whatever losses or hurts might occur. This was new ground for me. Surprisingly, I was less anxious and angry, more sure of myself and more trusting of my partner. I also know now that the love I get is given freely, not out of obligation.

I still need to grow in negotiating sex with my lover. It makes me anxious, shy, and vulnerable to ask for the sex I want. It is paradoxical to feel this way after a five-year relationship. My best guess is that the stakes are higher now. Time has increased the investment I have in him and with it I have increased my vulnerabilities. I would lose more now were I to lose him. And losing him at fifty-eight is different from losing him at thirty-five or forty-five or even fifty. Beyond this it seems, too, that shame about sex and sexuality may still lurk in the corners of my bedroom. I wonder if in this situation I am still working out the damage done by church and state, by school and family, work that will go on as long as church and state vilify gay sexuality. How many other gay men experience the same problem in their sexual relationships? Does this perhaps contribute to the decline of sexual activity and interest I hear about so often?

My answer to those questions focuses on my want and need for intimacy, and my belief that intimacy, particularly sexual intimacy, within a relationship of many years can arouse considerable anxiety. Being naked in heart and psyche as well as body before a man I love is daunting. It is not fear of abandonment alone that shakes me so. The risk of humiliation and shame and of disappointing my lover can turn me to stone. I know this is a major reason for my insisting on monogamy. If I am going to be that naked to someone, I need monogamy, or at least the sincere commitment to it. Having the boundaries secure around our relationship makes the anxiety of undressing much more tolerable. Otherwise, my anxiety spikes off the charts and I tend to mismanage matters.

There is one issue that has affected the endurance or abortion of my relationships. It is a circumstance that I believe is unique to all gay men—coming out. The extent to which I was closeted compromised the extent to which I could search for a suitable partner and the extent to which I could enjoy my relationship. The greater the difference between my partner and me on this measure, the greater the problems we experienced concerning sex, intimacy, family, and career. The problems resulting from the dissimilarity jeopardized the long-term viability of the relationship. In my first relationship I was fairly closeted. I met my first love in a gay bar. When we fell in love he challenged my uneasiness with my sexuality. He was right. I did my work and came out to everyone everywhere. But my coming out unmasked his ambivalence about homosexuality. It became a major block between us that affected everything from sex to shopping together as a couple.

I met my second lover in the Windy City Gay Chorus. He was as out as I was. The difficulties, which ultimately ended the relationship five years later, had less to do with coming out to others as such, as they did with ambivalence about homosexuality. I remember asking my lover to dance at a benefit where tony straights and gays gathered. "This is not the kind of event that gays dance at," I was told. "What kind of an event is the kind of event we can't dance at?" I retorted. We danced. Our differences were not so much about admitting to homosexuality as in living as full equals with heterosexuals.

I met my third and current partner at his restaurant in Chicago's Lincoln Park through my best friend. Very comfortable with his gay self, he was out in every quarter of his life. Our dissensions emanate from differences in circumstances such as age, comfort with conflict, and life experience. They are never about how openly gay we should be. I relish his speaking up whenever people make an errant homophobic remark. I love that he will kiss me goodbye at the airport or walk with his arm around my thickening waist in the park. Our relationship is a harbor where I need not fear the storms of homophobia.

To be sure, there were many issues that drove me to separate from my first two partners. But I think that the degree to which we were comfortable being gay influenced every other aspect of our relationships from sexual intimacy to negotiating budgets to deciding whose family to spend Christmas with or simply to dressing for an evening out. No more wasted energies arguing over who will wear the black jeans because of concerns about how it would look if we both wore them! No more denying who we are and what we are.

ENDING

And then she thought
you went on living one day after another
and in time you were somebody else,
your previous self only like a close relative,
a sister or brother, with whom you shared a past.
But a different person, a separate life.

Charles Frazier, *Cold Mountain*[3]

I have changed. I had to change. In many ways I am a stranger to my former self. I cringe at old photos that conjure up the constricted, repressed, and depressed life I was leading. People tell me now that I am younger than I was. I tell them I lived my old age first. When I came out, I broke the logjam that stifled my growth and embezzled my happiness. No more do I war inside, obsessing whether gay is good or good enough. No more wondering if God condemns my love and desire for men. Though scarred by homophobia, I no longer believe that I can never be happy because of it. My happiness resides finally within me and not in how much society, straight or gay, accepts me. Since coming out, I feel I belong in this world.

I would never go back to my teen years or to my twenties or thirties. It's been too hard to get here. Nor would I exchange for the exuberance of youth or beauty of body, not even for all the unbridled sex, the measure of wisdom and balance the striving of those years has given me. But I would like to talk to that younger man. I would tell him that there was never anything really wrong with him. In fact, much was good and right in him. The world was not ready for him or others like him. But I can't; time has closed that door. Instead I will tell other young men—in my work as a therapist, in the classes I teach, and in my friendships.

But while I am happy for the world I have built, I feel regret and loss for those I left behind in the process. I think this goes beyond the balancing of books that everyone does in the middle years. That balancing is a timely check to make the most of one's remaining years. But as a gay man, I experienced many losses of friendship as consequences of embracing my homosexuality. I could not find happiness in a straight dream or in approximating it or in a dream referenced to a straight society. I had to immigrate to a world where there were gay dreams. This world was hidden from straight eyes but embedded in their world. I couldn't live stretched between these two worlds and chose one. But, oh, how bitter was the loss. For, while I succeeded in finding or fashioning a happy home in a gay world, I abandoned and hurt people who loved me when I very much needed their love and affection. The recent funeral of a once-cherished straight friend conjured up the gulf between us because of our different sexual lives, a gulf widened not because of diminished love or resistance to change, but because twenty or thirty years ago, there was no way for our different worlds to blend. I struggle now to repair those relationships, but fear that our love may have grown too tired with neglect to recapture the affection and intimacy. It is, perhaps, the irony of these late middle years that with less time now there is greater need for reconciliation.

At the same time, I would be very remiss not to acknowledge extraordinary support from friends who are not gay. Their friendships have sustained me and enriched my life deeply. I have never understood why most of them are women. Perhaps it is because I identify more with them than I do with men. Perhaps it is because they evidenced the qualities of compassion and empathy I found lacking in men.

I want to continue to change. I want to be even more open about who I am, about what I want, and what I truly believe. Fear of abandonment still grips me at times. Then I shrink and shrivel like a penis in frigid waters. I forget everything I know about myself. Worse, I feel like a four-year-old, vulnerable and unable to take care of myself. I never want to experience that childhood disappointment or abandonment again, that rude rejection which says you are queer and it's your fault. It seems that fear and anxiety will always be my trick knee. Whenever or wherever I feel stress, it is this trick knee that acts up or gives out. But I know now how to face the fear more effectively. I literally remind myself that I am not that child but a mature man quite able to take care of himself, and that perhaps I am about to learn something that will improve my world.

And always there is AIDS. It continues to chill me. I think about death a lot. It has kept me centered on making the life I live rich and meaningful. But having contemporaries wither and fall to AIDS like so many leaves in a sudden autumn wind was a shock that has remained difficult to absorb. It sobered me, forced changes in my behavior, made every healthy breath I took more precious and tenuous. Having lived through the untimely deaths of contemporaries, I now face the timely deaths of parents and uncles and aunts and older friends. Death with its chilling caprice keeps peeling away the layers of protection. I feel naked to death. Despite it I feel full of life and in love with it, and remain bright with the prospect of more living tomorrow. But I do so knowing that I remain powerless to alter the least fact of living and dying. I can only cooperate, accept, and move with events. I can work. I can care. I can love, as mightily as my energies will allow. At fifty-eight, I find myself, like so many others in midlife, mystified between the living and the leaving.

NOTES

1. Ball, E. (1999). *Slaves in the Family* (p. 289). New York: Random House.

2. Carter, J. (1998). *The Virtues of Aging* (p. ix). New York: Ballantine Books.

3. Frasier, C. (1998). *Cold Mountain: A Novel* (p. 422). New York: Vintage Books.

Order Your Own Copy of
This Important Book for Your Personal Library!

GAY MEN AT MIDLIFE
Age Before Beauty

_____in hardbound at $49.95 (ISBN: 1-56023-979-4)

_____in softbound at $17.95 (ISBN: 1-56023-980-8)

COST OF BOOKS_____

OUTSIDE USA/CANADA/
MEXICO: ADD 20%____

POSTAGE & HANDLING_____
(US: $4.00 for first book & $1.50
for each additional book)
Outside US: $5.00 for first book
& $2.00 for each additional book)

SUBTOTAL_____

in Canada: add 7% GST____

STATE TAX____
(NY, OH & MIN residents, please
add appropriate local sales tax)

FINAL TOTAL____
(If paying in Canadian funds,
convert using the current
exchange rate, UNESCO
coupons welcome.)

❑ **BILL ME LATER:** ($5 service charge will be added)
(Bill-me option is good on US/Canada/Mexico orders only;
not good to jobbers, wholesalers, or subscription agencies.)

❑ Check here if billing address is different from
shipping address and attach purchase order and
billing address information.

Signature_____

❑ **PAYMENT ENCLOSED:** $_____

❑ **PLEASE CHARGE TO MY CREDIT CARD.**

❑ Visa ❑ MasterCard ❑ AmEx ❑ Discover
❑ Diner's Club ❑ Eurocard ❑ JCB

Account # _____

Exp. Date_____

Signature_____

Prices in US dollars and subject to change without notice.

NAME_____

INSTITUTION_____

ADDRESS_____

CITY_____

STATE/ZIP_____

COUNTRY_____ COUNTY (NY residents only)_____

TEL_____ FAX_____

E-MAIL_____

May we use your e-mail address for confirmations and other types of information? ❑ Yes ❑ No
We appreciate receiving your e-mail address and fax number. Haworth would like to e-mail or fax special
discount offers to you, as a preferred customer. **We will never share, rent, or exchange your e-mail address
or fax number.** We regard such actions as an invasion of your privacy.

Order From Your Local Bookstore or Directly From
The Haworth Press, Inc.
10 Alice Street, Binghamton, New York 13904-1580 • USA
TELEPHONE: 1-800-HAWORTH (1-800-429-6784) / Outside US/Canada: (607) 722-5857
FAX: 1-800-895-0582 / Outside US/Canada: (607) 722-6362
E-mail: getinfo@haworthpressinc.com
PLEASE PHOTOCOPY THIS FORM FOR YOUR PERSONAL USE.
www.HaworthPress.com

BOF00